"What awesome revela _____ ___ into the mind and heart of a former prodigal. Pastor Danny's openness and transparency about his life experiences give us firsthand knowledge into how and why someone who is raised in church by godly parents can turn away from God. More importantly, his book gives parents hope that no matter how impossible things might look, God's Word never leaves. For parents who look to Proverbs 22:6 as God's promise for their children, this book, *Through the Eyes of a Prodigal,* reinforces that promise."

—Pastor Richard Salazar
Senior Pastor, New Harvest Norwalk

"In my twenty-three years of pastoring, seeing someone walk away from the faith is one of the most gut-wrenching experiences I've had to endure. When that person is your own offspring, the pain is multiplied. Danny is one of those rare gems who has found his way back and is now pursuing those who are still far from God. He has the insight to lend hope to those who are on the outside looking in as well as parents whose children have strayed. I believe if you open your heart to these firsthand accounts of someone who once was in the pig pen, God will breathe fresh energy into your soul."

—Tom Watson
Pastor, San Pedro, California

"*Through the Eyes of a Prodigal* is an eye-opening account of a common problem in the church today that is rarely discussed. Church kids raised to know the truth have it all yet risk it all by leaving the church to experience temporary fulfillment in the world. Here you have a personal account which brings to light the serious issues facing church kids today. It is a must-read for all ages."

—George Zendejas
Vision Leader of Ignite the Foothills
Young Adults Ministry, Azusa, California

THROUGH THE EYES OF A PRODIGAL

HOPE FOR PARENTS AND LEADERS WITH WAYWARD CHILDREN

DANNY CASAS JR.

WESTBOW
PRESS
A DIVISION OF THOMAS NELSON

WestBow Press books may be ordered through booksellers or by contacting:

WestBow Press
A Division of Thomas Nelson
1663 Liberty Drive
Bloomington, IN 47403
www.westbowpress.com
1-(866) 928-1240

ISBN: 978-1-4497-5452-5 (sc)
ISBN: 978-1-4497-5453-2 (e)

Library of Congress Control Number: 2012909533

Printed in the United States of America

WestBow Press rev. date: 06/11/2012

DEDICATION

To my beautiful wife, Sabrina, for being everything I dreamed of and so much more. I am truly blessed to have you standing at my side. You're the best, baby girl.

CONTENTS

FOREWORD

I began reading *Through the Eyes of a Prodigal* as we were flying over the Atlantic Ocean on our way to England, and it contained such valuable information, with a great amount of power and hope for every parent. As I was reading, it took me way back to when I stumbled across a few of his writings. This book is proof that God is raising up a new kind of writer for this generation—and Danny is one of them. He and his wife, Sabrina, at the young age of twenty-four, answered the call to take over a church in Porterville, California. He comes from the breed of the prodigal, and because of that, he's able to release inspiration to parents. He is one who knows the God of Abraham, Isaac, and Jacob, and because of that, there is an open heaven with insight and power released into his life. This, in turn, releases hope into the hearts of prodigal parents.

Daniel Casas, Sr.
Pastor
New Harvest Christian Fellowship of Fresno

Acknowledgments

First and foremost, thanks to my Lord and Savior, Jesus Christ.

To my parents, Daniel and Barbara Casas. This project certainly wouldn't be possible without you both. Thank you for believing in me and teaching me to serve the Lord.

To Roy and Virginia Jaramillo for blessing me with such a wonderful wife!

To my sons, Daniel, Noah, and Nehemiah and to my little princess, Zeriah. Dad loves you guys!

To my sisters, Jennifer, Christina, and Jazzy. You ladies are the best little sisters a guy could have.

Much love also to my grandmothers, Elvita Rivas and Esther Fernandez. Thanks for all your help, support, and home-cooked meals throughout the years!

A special thanks to Pastor Richard and Sister Nancy Salazar. Your leadership and impact on countless lives, including mine, will never be forgotten.

And to every parent who still believes God will return his or her prodigal.

INTRODUCTION

Years ago, God planted in my heart an idea to write a book on prodigals. Writing a book is like putting a huge puzzle together. Piece after piece, month after month, and page after page, a book started to slowly unfold. The more I wrote, the more I was pressed to get this book in the hands of others who were in circumstances similar to the ones that I placed my family in.

I was a prodigal, but now I am a pastor who carries a heavy burden for wayward young people. I grew up in a good Christian family with great parents. My father is a minister, and my mother is an intercession leader. But in spite of all this, I still turned away from the Lord. I share my story and experiences to encourage parents, leaders, and close friends that no one is beyond God's saving grace. I would even go as far as saying that the purpose of this book can be summed up with two words—reigniting hope.

In this book, I cover a range of topics that people with prodigals encounter. More importantly, you'll find vital answers or key pieces that will assist and support you in this journey. We begin the book by focusing on the classic story of the lost son found in the gospel of Luke.

In chapter 1, we cover the journey of a prodigal and look at six key places all prodigals travel through.

In the next chapter, I tell my story. This story will validate my message and also provide inspiration to parents of rebellious church kids.

In chapters three and four, we look at the pain that wayward sons and daughters bring to their parents and close with a great emphasis on how to regain hope in the midst of trying times.

In one of my favorite chapters, "Reaching Your Prodigal," I talk about four significant points that were instrumental in my return. Following that is "The Power of Your Words." In this section, I present a biblical perspective and personal stories of how our tongues are extremely powerful—particularly when speaking to prodigals.

I also want to speak to parents who still have tweens or teens in the house. It is completely obvious that our generation of young people is facing unparalleled challenges that assault the roots of their faith. Christian parents must be aware of the fiery darts that the enemy has pointed at the hearts and minds of their children. In each chapter, you'll find information relevant to that battle.

Chapters seven and eight were written specifically for parents with pre-teens and teenagers. The ninth chapter is entitled "For Prodigals Only." In this section, I answer some very important questions and arguments that prodigals hold.

We conclude the book with "Heaven's Heroes," in which we examine everyday heroes who are on the frontlines, battling for the souls of their prodigals. We look at their spiritual investment from an eternal outlook. It's really encouraging.

I pray that this book blesses you and is a valuable tool to help you on your journey in rearing your youth. I believe that this book will spark a new flame and passion in hurting parents and leaders who have lost their children to the world. It's also my hope that God uses the pages of this book to provide critical answers to many of the questions that some of you encounter regarding your children. Moreover, my desire is that these pages touch the lives of your wayward son or daughter directly. If one sentence, paragraph, or chapter is used by God to bring him or her to Christ, then my investment was well worth it!

Let's get started, reading one page at time with an open heart. Together, we will complete one of the most difficult puzzles that life brings—the puzzle of reaching your prodigal.

The Journey of Prodigals

Not long after that, the younger son got together all he had, set off for a distant country and there squandered his wealth in wild living. Luke 15:13

THE BACK DOOR OF THE church has become a familiar exit for countless young people. A generation of church kids finds its members uprooting from the fresh soil of their local sanctuary to find greener pastures in the world. The stats on the church dropout rate after high school are staggering. One major denomination even reported that "88 percent of the children raised in evangelical homes leave church at the age of eighteen."[1]

These kids aren't just any kids; they're home-grown church kids who have been blessed all throughout their childhood and adolescences with the gospel. They learn about Jesus in the nursery, Sunday school, and youth group only to face their first tastes of freedom and choose to abandon Christ for the cheap pleasures of sin. Consequently, their actions hurt everyone who comes in the cross fire, such as

---

[1] "Family Council says it's time to bring the family back to life," Jon Walker, accessed May 18, 2012, http://www.sbcannualmeeting. net/sbc02/newsroom/newspage.asp

their parents, pastors, and friends. The collateral damage that follows their trail of waywardness is beyond belief.

Who Do Prodigals Hurt?

First considering the effect of prodigals on the church. Nothing hurts more than having a young person who you have seen grow up leave God and destroy his or her destiny in Christ. When a wayward son or daughter leaves it's usually never on good terms. Adding insult to injury, most times, these children wag their fingers at everyone who invested in their future as they leave. As a pastor, it's very painful to see young people with so much promise waste their lives on temporary things that carry such a high price tag. It's also insulting to closely witness the methods and measures they use to accomplish their exodus from the church.

Secondly, prodigals hurt their families. Take a look at the influence of prodigals on their families; this influence is discouraging. The hurt and pain that flows from the eyes of their fathers and mothers cannot be hidden. Many are embarrassed, dishonored, and devastated. The actions of their children are like sharp daggers to their hearts.

Thirdly, they hurt themselves. Prodigals fail to recognize that their futures are at stake. All are living for the present day—for possession and passion. They do not fully grasp how their actions are going to ruin them. Hopelessness, emptiness, and endless searching permeate the future of every prodigal who I have come to know.

Lastly, they hurt God. Not only does the prodigal hurt the church, family, and himself or herself, but he or she also ultimately hurts God. The most important person is the one who prodigals fail to take into account. All throughout Scripture, we see that God is a faithful and loving Father. As believers, we all know personally that we serve a God who intimately cares about His children. When prodigals hurt, God hurts; it's as simple as that.

THE STORY OF THE PRODIGAL SON

One of the most compelling stories in the entire Bible is the story of the prodigal son. The parable is about a young man who took his inheritance only to leave home and squander it all in wild living and unwise choices. Finally, after losing everything, he came to his wits end. He sold himself as a slave and was reduced to feeding pigs. Remembering his father's house, he decided to journey back and seek forgiveness from his father. On his way home, his father saw him from afar. Instead of holding a grudge against his son for his foolishness, the father was ready and willing to forgive his repentant son.

In this powerful story, we see the heart of God. We see His unending love for the lost, and we also find that He desires to restore prodigals back to their rightful place in His kingdom. As in all of scripture, God gives us this story for a divine reason—to supply needed inspiration. Looking closely at this parable, we discover six places where the lost son and all prodigals sometimes find themselves. In these places, we find a wealth of revelation to help them make it back to the Father's house.

THE FATHER'S HOUSE

We begin with the best place by far, which is the father's house. Imagine a huge house set in a beautiful countryside. The house has spacious rooms, the finest furniture, and most notably, the father. Laughter fills the rooms, and joy resonates from the walls in this home. The atmosphere is one that reflects the head of household—the father. The peace of his protection, the joy of his presence, and the provisions that he provides all reveal his love.

This home of the prodigal represents the church and its environment today—all that it encompasses, such as learning about Christ, growing up with other believers, and experiencing God. These all are things that church kids experience as they grow up in the Father's house— the church.

But as with the prodigal son, it seems that the familiarity of the father's house can cause church kids to be unaware of how good they have it. The attitude of some is that they are missing out on the action and fun of the world. As a result, they're ungrateful for what they have.

When I was a young teen, I played basketball with an older gentleman who attended the church where my father ministered. After the game, we went out for some food. He began telling me about the mistakes that he had made as a young man. With a serious look in his eyes, he almost pleaded with me not to follow in his footsteps and warned me to make right choices in my life. He was trying to tell me to change my attitude. At the time, I didn't realize the priceless things that I had, like being spared from the pain that sin brings and having two parents who truly loved God and me.

I wanted freedom, and as a result, I was blinded to the blessings that were right in front of my face. This all happened because I thought—like many church kids do—that I was missing out, when in actuality, I was only missing out on things that I could've really done without. This is the bait that Satan used to push me to the next location that prodigals travel.

THE JOURNEY FROM HOME

"Not long after that, the younger son got together all he had, set off for a distant country" (Luke 15:13).

Picture a young man gathering his belongings and getting ready to journey far from home. I can see his father wishing his son final goodbyes as tears run down his face. This would be the last time his dad would see him for a very long time. The prodigal had a long journey through the dry desert to a distant country, where he would learn a great but painful lesson about life without his father.

The journey from home leads to the place where the heart of a prodigal is fully persuaded that God isn't the right fit for him or her in the future. This case of spiritual apathy in their lives doesn't necessarily mean that a child will pack his or her bags and leave the house immediately, as the prodigal son did. However, it will be apparent, by a child's attitude at church and home that his or her heart is out the door. There are many things that contribute to this. Here are several that I've heard and seen personally.

Prodigals follow their so-called friends. The apostle Paul wrote, "Bad company corrupts good character" (1 Corinthians 15:33). Bad friends have a powerful way of influencing the choices and attitudes of your children. As a result of these bad choices, good kids turn to bad kids, and bad kids turn worse. There is a transferring power in the people we are associated with—both for the positive and negative. A lot of times, church kids end up idolizing the new kid or the rebellious kids at school and at church only to be negatively influenced or even controlled by that person.

Prodigals are influenced by the media. Ten years ago, we thought that things couldn't get worse in regards to media—but they have. Just look at how Christian young people in the public arena are mocked for their faith and purity. Recently, NFL quarterback Tim Tebow, who is an outspoken Christian, was mocked for his faith on NBC's *Saturday Night Live.* Tebow was portrayed as a dimwitted religious zealot in front of millions of people—many of them young people.

The enemy's agenda is to pessimistically corrupt or mislead church kids via media—and it is an effective strategy.

The media consumption of today's youth is revealed by their attitude, desires, and disdain for all that is godly. We are what we eat. The same is true for our media diet, which is the TV programming that we consume with our eyes and ears. Kids with unhealthy media diets are going to be unhealthy from a spiritual standpoint. Many are influenced out of church because they are consumed by a system in which God is mocked or simply doesn't exist.

Prodigals make sexual mistakes and have sexual misconceptions. Sadly, the sex drives of many young people are pulling them away from the things of God. I know of many people who have left the church because of sexual mistakes. But I have also been privileged to witness some stand strong against the waves of sexual pressure, and the blessings that have followed them have made their wait for sex well worth it. Others haven't been as blessed—or to be more accurate, they haven't been as wise. Bad sexual choices contrary to God's Word have opened the floodgates to a lot of negatives. Those consequences could have been avoided if young people listened to what they were taught from the pulpit and by the good example of others.

Prodigals have pride. Proverbs 16:18 says, "Pride goes before destruction, a haughty spirit before a fall." How is pride connected with church kids leaving God? Well, pride blinds them to the truth. In the life of a prodigal, pride usually plays out like this: you try to show your child that he or she is going down the wrong road, making terrible decisions that are going to ruin his or her future, and the response is, "Yeah, I know." They really have no clue, but they believe they do.

The journey out the door usually falls in these categories, but it is in no way limited to these factors. Like you, I have heard many different reasons and excuses why people leave God, but a greater part is somehow rooted in these.

THE PENTHOUSE

"The younger son got together all he had, set off for a distant country and there squandered his wealth in wild living" (Luke 15:13).

The prodigal son wasn't leaving home to live a pious life in a mountain convent; he was leaving home to have a taste of the wild side. The modern-day equivalent to what he experienced would be if you gave your kid a big sum of your life savings, and then your child drove off in a new sports car to Las Vegas!

Finally, the prodigal arrives at the destination that he's been longing for. I can imagine him stumbling as he gets off of his donkey with a pocket full of cash, ready to live it up. He found himself in the place that he had wanted to be for so long. The place all prodigals find themselves in for a short season is the penthouse.

The penthouse can be defined as the place where prodigals experience firsthand that sin is fun and pleasurable. This is the climax of all their planning and forethought. In this place, the soul is merry and careless. The future looks electrifying, and everyone who opposed their decisions seems closed-minded and old-fashioned. It's where prodigals get haughty and brazen-faced against all their teachers. They come to church, walking and talking with an attitude and swagger like they own the place. They joke with anyone who will listen to their garbage. At this time, prodigals feel like they're on top of the world—their first taste of freedom, they reason. They think they know exactly what they are talking about and that everyone else—including God—was wrong.

I must also mention that the only way anyone can get to the penthouse is by constantly pushing the mute button on the voice of God. I'm sure that as the prodigal son left home, his dad told him, "Son, do the right thing. Remember what I taught you about life, and most importantly, honor God." This is what many good Christian parents tell their children as they come of age. Finally, the lost son heard his last lecture from his father. His bags were packed; it was time to head down to sin city. Thinking that he finally escaped the truth, on some dusty road in route to his destination, amidst all the voices of sin, he heard a still, small voice whispering, *Turn back. Don't do it. You don't belong here.* But instead of listening, he continued down that wide road.

At this point—only after faithful warnings—does God give people over to their passions and desires (Romans 1:24). God has given all people the choice to serve Him or not, but before they can walk out on Him, He will always give them ample warning of what this choice can cause. In the life of every prodigal, God does this. The warnings come from all different places, people, and even circumstances. After rejecting the warnings, there comes a short time when the voice of truth subsides momentarily. Many prodigals in this place truly believe that they are the exception to the rule—God's rule, that is. They reason that the pleasures they experience are the indictor of this. Recently, I read a *Dear Abby* article that shows what many prodigals in the penthouse perceive of their parent's biblical views.

> Dear Abby, I'm twenty-three, the only child of a controlling, paranoid, hermitlike, and hyperreligious mother and a peace-loving, passive father. I graduated from college last year. Shortly after, my boyfriend and I accepted dream jobs in the same town several hours away from my parents. Mom was appalled. She warned me that I wouldn't last and would come home. Instead, I have embraced my new city and job. Mom is at her wit's end. When I mentioned that my boyfriend had recorded a movie for me, she said he was controlling me via technology. She calls me constantly, and if I don't answer, she leaves frantic messages about how disrespectful I am and how she and Dad are praying for my soul.[2]

---

[2]   Van Buren, Abigail. "Daughter could use counseling to cope with controlling mom." *Chicago Sun-Times,* January 16, 2012.

No doubt the penthouse is the apex of spiritual blindness, as seen with this wayward young woman. Even though prodigals truly believe that they are finally free, it's quite the opposite. They're in the deepest bondage ever. In this state, parents are treated like they need to be admitted into a psych ward. Pastors are deemed as "haters." Everyone who doesn't take the prodigal's side is considered crazy and closed-minded. Please remember that eventually, the fun is going to end. It may take months or years, but a prodigal's next destination will validate all the warnings that you gave him or her.

THE PIG'S PEN

"After he had spent everything, there was a severe famine in that whole country, and he began to be in need. So he went and hired himself out to a citizen of that country, who sent him to his fields to feed pigs" (Luke 15:14-15).

When I think about the pig's pen, I see a hot wasteland and a tattered old barn sitting right in the middle of it, full of dirty, disease-infected swine. In the center of this desolate place is a famished, penniless boy who lost everything he ever had—including his dignity. No doubt, this is an ugly place to be. It's where reality sets in and fantasy fades away. All the so-called friends are gone, all the fun is gone, and complete emptiness pierces the soul.

The young person finds that what parents and spiritual leaders warned about was not because they were trying to make life miserable, but rather to save him from the wretchedness of this place. He discovers that all parties come to a dreadful end and finds himself wishing that he would have listened to his teachers. The voice of their warnings plays over and over in his head like a depressing song on repeat. The missed opportunities, unheeded advice, and monumental choices flash over and over in his mind, haunting him.

When we examine the prodigal in Luke's gospel, we see that a severe famine seized the land. In his state of need, the prodigal resorted to selling himself to a local famer just to eat. This once-prosperous and protected son, who was highly valued by his father, became a slave to a foreigner. His occupation was feeding pigs! From the penthouse to the pig house, sin doesn't have a gradual slope. The fall of a prodigal is like getting pulled out of warm water and thrown into frigid currents. The lost soul goes from one extreme to the next, and the longer she decides to stay in the pig's pen, the more intense the misery becomes.

This story shows that humility at times comes from being humiliated. Brokenness comes from being broken. And godly repentance comes to those who God disciplines. But even in these circumstances, we see the finger of God allowing this to transpire so that His purposes might emerge. In the mist of the madness, the prodigal hears a soft, gentle whisper of a loving father. The voice comes to the heart of the wayward soul and says, *I still love you*. This is the heart cry of heaven. When all are gone, there is one who remains—the one who never left. And this is the impetus to journey home.

THE JOURNEY BACK HOME

"When he came to his senses, he said, 'How many of my father's hired men have food to spare, and here I am starving to death! I will set out and go back to my father and say to him: Father, I have sinned against heaven and against you. I am no longer worthy to be called your son; make me like one of your hired men.' So he got up and went to his father" (Luke 15:17-20).

Finally, it happened. The prodigal son had enough. The journey back home can be defined as the turnaround. The soul comes to its senses and realizes its desperate need for repentance before God and others. The prodigal is driven here by guilt, want, and need; nevertheless, he is pushed to his knees for a divine reason—return! There are three parallels between this ancient prodigal and today's prodigal. Certain things will drive prodigals back home if they are willing to humble themselves.

Prodigals long for food. Although this young man hungered for physical food, prodigals long for spiritual food. Many prodigals in the pig's pen think about being in church and recall the sermons that they heard from their pastors. They think about familiar jokes, poignant stories, activities, campouts, gatherings, and fellowship that taught them the Word of God. And this message doesn't return void (Isaiah 55:11).

Prodigals want their clothes back. People living in sin who once lived for Christ know that their clothes are toiled and stinky. The prodigal son wore dirty, smelly rags in the pig's pen. His situation was opposite of "rags to riches"; he went from riches to rags. We find that prodigals have this longing. Even if they wear some really nice clothes externally, they wear dilapidated garments internally. Shame and guilt from sin has a way of wearing down on a person like a moth has a way of wearing down a garment. A life full of holes follows—although the holes cannot be seen physically, they do exist.

Prodigals long to be with Dad. Yet another impetus for return is the presence of the Father. While in the pig's pen, of all the places in the world, this boy started to remember his father's house. He thought about the rooms that he grew up in and the joy of being with his father. Likewise, in the life of today's prodigal, once she tastes the presence of God, nothing in the entire world can supply the same satisfaction. Nothing can come remotely close. For prodigals, this is the main reason for return. The presence of God draws them home.

BACK IN THE FATHER'S HOUSE

"The son said to him, 'Father, I have sinned against heaven and against you. I am no longer worthy to be called your son.' But the father said to his servants, 'Quick! Bring the best robe and put it on him. Put a ring on his finger and sandals on his feet. Bring the fattened calf and kill it. Let's have a feast and celebrate. For this son of mine was dead and is alive again; he was lost and is found.' So they began to celebrate" (Luke 15:21-24).

When I think about the prodigal's arrival back to his dad's house, I can't help but wonder why the Bible says that his father saw him from a long way off (Luke 15:20). The picture Jesus painted is of a father who waited on, prayed for, and believed in his son's return.

What we find in this divine meeting arranged by heaven is truly powerful. There are two elements that we'll always see when someone comes back to the Father's house. One is true repentance, and another is God's restoration.

1. *True Repentance* The prodigal admitted that he was wrong and acknowledged that he sinned against heaven and his father. The perquisite for a person to return to the father's house is repentance. Without true repentance, someone cannot be restored. He cannot be truly changed until he is willing to turn away from his sinful lifestyle, admit his sins, and then forsake them. Genuine repentance is a beautiful thing. It's more than tears, promises, or telling your wrongdoings to another. True repentance is a change of heart. After this occurrence, a new person is born. A humble and thankful man or woman emerges.

2. *God's Restoration* After the prodigal son repented to God and his father, his dad received him again. One of the greatest benefits of repentance is God's restoration. The father began to give back what the enemy had stolen from his son.

The first thing that was restored was their relationship. "His father saw him and was filled with compassion for him; he ran to his son, threw his arms around him and kissed him" (Luke 15:20). This is symbolic of a sinner coming back and God receiving her. We can all agree that it's an awesome thing to be forgiven by the Lord and restored back to right standing with God.

Secondly, the extravagant father said, "Put a ring on his hand." In ancient times, giving a ring was a sign of dignity and honor (Genesis 41:42). Prodigals who repent and leave their sins get their dignity back. The past guilt and shame is washed away, and the dignity that is found in Christ is restored.

Lastly, the father told one of his servants to "put some sandals on his feet" (Luke 15:22). His son's feet were dirty and callused from the long journey without shoes, just as prisoners' feet would have been. During this era, captives walked shoeless. The shoes represent deliverance from captivity. Yes, repentance opens the door for liberty.

Conclusion

When I look back at these six places, I relive my past. I'm reminded of being in the father's house as a young boy only to let my selfishness pull me away from God. I even recall arriving at the penthouse and thinking that I was on top of the world. I also remember how that world shattered my life. But in all of my memories, the greatest was when I returned home. The love that showered me that day is reminiscent of when the prodigal son was embraced by his dad. Nothing in the entire world could explain what I felt; mere words can't come close. But if there was one word I had to choose, it would be *love*—God's undying, undeserved, *agape* love. This is the love that pursues your prodigal. This is the love that gives us reason to believe that someday, our children will make it home.

My Story

"For I know the plans I have for you," declares the Lord,
"plans to prosper you and not to harm you, plans to give
you hope and a future." Jeremiah 29:11

A FEW YEARS AGO, MY wife and I vacationed with some friends down in San Diego. One friend started talking to me about when I was a teenager. The conversion was going great until he blurted out something that really caught my attention. He said, "Wow, I can't believe you're a pastor now! I never would have thought; you were so lost."

My friend's words caught me by surprise. Had I forgotten how far God brought me? Or maybe I never fully realized how lost I was. He wasn't the only one who has told me that over the years. Time and time again, people come up to me and say, "I remember you when you weren't saved, and by no means would I have guessed that you would have given your life over to Christ." It's really embarrassing when it happens, but when I think about what these people are saying, their words make complete sense. I was lost; my heart, words, and actions all were overwhelming evidence to that sad reality.

Honestly, if you knew me when I was fifteen years old, you probably wouldn't have predicted that I would be a pastor. You may have thought I'd be a drunk or a drug-using vagabond, but I definitely wasn't going to be voted "most likely to succeed in ministry." I was voted "wildest party animal" at one youth gathering—seriously.

In no way am I writing this to give glory to my past or impress anyone. I'm writing this to bless someone who thinks there is no hope—someone who is on the brink of giving up. I write for someone who has bought into the lie that her son is too deep in sin or that his daughter is past all grace and will never return home. My life and the lives of other prodigals testify that the game isn't over yet. God's into late-game comebacks—prodigal comebacks.

Truly, my life story isn't the most dramatic. It might be pretty bland depending on your point of view. For example, I've never been in jail—or arrested, for that matter. I've never robbed a bank or been in a high-speed car chase. I haven't done a lot of things that might spice up this chapter a bit.

For the most part, my story isn't uncommon for a church kid. When I say "church kid," that's exactly what my sisters and I were. I was homeschooled since the second grade and went to church over a hundred times a year (I am not exaggerating). I played the drums for worship before my feet could reach the pedals—not in Sunday school, but in the big show. I was baptized three or four times—I can't remember. My father is a pastor. My mother is a pastor's wife. Do I really need to say any more?

From the earliest time of my life, my whole world revolved around church. I was even dedicated to the Lord as infant. In front of the congregation, I was dressed like a baby preacher, and my life was handed over to the Lord for His purpose and glory. My parents surrendered the keys of my destiny over to the Creator, and when I ran from God, this one act of faith always seemed to haunt me—for the good, of course.

Both of my parents were saved at the tail end of the Jesus movement in Los Angeles. They came from broken backgrounds and found true and lasting hope for the first time in their lives. Thirty years later, their lives bear witness to the power of Jesus. They met in church, had the same goal of reaching the world for Christ, and most importantly, were attracted to each other. They decided to get married. I was the first of four—their only boy. I was followed by my three wonderful sisters, Jennifer, Christina, and Jasmine.

THE WINDY CITY

My dad and mom were heavily involved in ministry at their home church from the time they gave their lives to Jesus in the late '70s. When I was five years old, my parents answered the call to pastor in Chicago. We uprooted from sunny southern California and embarked on a four-day drive in our little white car from the West Coast to the

Midwest to pioneer a church in the heart of the Windy City.

The moment we arrived, my parents set out to reach anyone who would listen. Back in the late '80s, Chicago's crime was off the charts, and our church was right in the middle of it. My parents ministered to people who, for the most part, many wouldn't want to sit next to at church. Pimps, prostitutes, thugs, and drug addicts were all welcome inside the doors of our tiny brick storefront building located on 47th and Ashland. No one was ever rejected. In the four years that we were there, I saw both of my parents labor in love, sacrifice in tears, and stand by faith, even though the crowds were small and the finances were tight.

As a kid, I prayed a lot for God to bring people to my dad's church in Chicago. I guess my prayers stemmed from the fact that our church was so little and their dreams were so big. I remember times when the only people in our church were my parents and my two sisters. (My youngest sister, Jazz, hadn't be born yet.) We were very excited when we had a full house of visitors. There were times when I asked my mom why our church was so small, and she said, "Just pray, son."

Once, my mother and I were in my dad's office, and we overheard a visitor walking through the doors during one of our midweek services to be greeted by my father. We were very excited. My dad asked him what his name was, and he said, "Elvis." My father inquired what his last name was, and to our amazement, he uttered, "Presley." Even more shocking was the fact that he never said that he was joking. This man even had Elvis's notorious leg-shaking routine that he performed from time to time!

My mom and I tried to control our laughter, but I'm sure that he overheard us. So for the next couple of months, my father had a new disciple—none other than the one and only Elvis Presley. I guess my prayers did something. And believe me when I say that even as a seven-year-old, I was willing to do anything that I could to help the church grow. When my family arrived before church, I would walk to the left side of our one-step altar, get on my knees, and beg God to bring people in. Sometimes it worked; at others times, it didn't. Regardless of how things turned out during that particular service, I learned how to pray.

About three months before we left Chicago to come back to California, I was in my bedroom in the middle of the night and was prompted to pray. But this time was totally different from all the other times at the altar. It was around 3:00 a.m., and I was wide awake. As a kid, I was never was wide awake in the night. But this time, for some mysterious reason, I got out of my bed and began pacing my first-floor apartment room, fully conscious.

I don't remember what I was praying for, but something different happened! The best way to describe it is that I felt as though a window from heaven was opened that I never knew existed. I began to weep and utter things I could not normally express. It was like a river from heaven was being poured into the deepest parts of my soul. It was a river that was living, fresh, and beyond description. It's hard to describe that experience; I almost feel that I'm doing a disservice attempting to. That night was the first of several encounters I had with the Holy Spirit.

BACK IN CALIFORNIA

After four years of chilly winters, there was an opportunity for my parents to lead a church back in central California. This time, we exchanged the below-zero temperatures of the Midwest for the triple-digit heat of Fresno, California. Again, we packed our bags and answered the call.

The first few years in Fresno were exciting for me. My parents finally started to see the natural fruition of all their labors in Chicago. The worship was moving, evangelism was outstanding, and people came to Christ. My dad was a full-time pastor, and our church had a school, so my sisters and I spent a good part of our day at the church.

Because we were there so often, my sisters and I had to come up with creative ways to entertain ourselves while our parents tended to the needs of the church. We even played "church"—probably because we were there so much. I was the preacher, and my sister, Jennifer, was the special guest singer. After she sang, she sat down with my sister, Christina, and they were my congregation. They were great—always receptive to my short messages that I would borrow from my father or other preachers I admired who spoke at our church. They shouted, "Amen, pastor!" as I expounded on whatever the latest heavy topic was. Even as a boy, when I preached to my little sisters and empty chairs, I knew that God had something ahead for me behind the pulpit.

The desire to preach stayed with me as I entered my preteen years. During one summer campout, I took a step that I would never forget. During an evening service, the camp leader spoke on answering God's "call." He even said that some of us boys would be pastors! He had a special altar invitation for all of us who felt called. In front of about two hundred young men, many of us took a bold step and went up for a special prayer. One young camp counselor met me at the altar and prayed for me with all of his heart. I wanted desperately be a pastor, and that night, I felt like God confirmed what I would later become.

People often ask me how I knew that I was called to preach. I always tell them about when I was a boy preaching to his little sisters and the empty chairs that surrounded them. Some understand; others look at me, puzzled. I truly feel that the call of God was planted in my heart as a boy. I never heard an audible voice saying, "My son, you will be a pastor!" But during those days, preaching to my sisters and during campout experiences, I knew I was called to preach. Someday, I would follow in my father's footsteps and be a pastor of a thriving church. In fact, even as a kid, I read my Bible, memorized Scriptures, fasted, and even evangelized with my father. I had the same desire as my dad and mom to see the world transformed by the power and love of Jesus. Too bad I didn't always stay that way.

MY SLOW DRIFT

Sadly, I slowly began to drift from being the kid who preached and prayed for his parents to the kid who drove his parents to pray. After about three years back in California, I started to change for the worst. Around age eleven, my downward spiral began. I guess the enemy knew it was time to attack my parents. And instead of using someone from the outside, he used someone from the inside.

It started off small. I began watching things on TV and listening to music that my parents would simply not allow. Then it progressed. I began stealing from stores, then vandalizing, then smoking cigarettes, then smoking weed, then using LSD, and a lot of others things that I am too ashamed to mention. I began skateboarding to have an excuse to leave the house. Let me make it clear that not all skaters are unruly, foul-mouthed drug users—but I was, and so were some of my friends. My life was going the opposite direction of what I was taught by my parents. I ran from God, and my heart hardened toward Him.

On one occasion, my father had a guest speaker come to our church and preach one Sunday morning. He was a great preacher. After the message, he began praying for people, and they cried and were touched by God. Then he looked around, looked directly at me, and called me up to the altar so he could pray for me. When he prayed, I felt like something was telling me to surrender. I heard another voice saying, "Don't listen; It's all a show."

Wretchedly, I listened to the enemy. I stood up there and put walls around my heart when he prayed. My attitude of resistance toward the Holy Spirit was pretty much the template of all my junior high and high school days.

A Bible character I can really relate to is Jonah. The prophet Jonah was commissioned by God to warn the city of Nineveh of God's impending judgment, but Jonah decided to skip town and catch a boat in the opposite direction. That was me. I went in the reverse direction of God's leading. You might ask, "Why? You grew up in church; you had great parents. God spared you from so much. Why would you want the world?" It really doesn't make sense. But the best answer I can give you is that I was selfish, bitter, and didn't know what I had.

I was selfish in wanting to know what sin felt like, and since it felt good, I wanted more. I was also bitter toward the church and God. I felt like the church had come between my parents and me all my life, so I was bent on getting even with them. I forgot how much the church had done for my family. Many people from the congregation reached out to me and blessed my parents and sisters. My eyes were blinded by rebellion; I looked at church from a skeptic's perspective. The deception only increased, and the pain of sin only grew. Confusion covered my mind like a dark cloud.

During those days, I remember waking up morning after morning with emptiness in my soul. I looked out my upstairs window at the fog that clouded the skyline and felt that my frame of mind was foggier. Life made no sense. I was in a maze, searching for contentment in things that only magnified the pain. I would grab my skateboard and exit the house, riding through the streets of the Tower District, looking for some dubious activity to engage in.

I never found what I was looking for. Even with friends, drugs, and alcohol, I felt all alone. After the buzz went away, I was back to being an empty teenager. As time progressed, so did the torment. There were some nights when suicidal thoughts flooded my mind because of the pain, confusion, and depression that I faced. I was overwhelmed to the point where I wanted to end it all. Thankfully, I never did.

Some young people think that it's easy to live a life of blatant disobedience to God. No, it's quite the opposite for anyone who has known Christ. God's truth leaves an indelible impression that you can never erase. This impression haunts a sinner. She can run from it, hide from it, and even reject it, but it's something she can never escape. The Bible says in Psalm 139:8-12,

> If I go up to the heavens, you are there; if I make my bed in the depths, you are there. If I rise on the wings of the dawn, if I settle on the far side of the sea, even there your hand will guide me, your right hand will hold me fast. If I say, "Surely the darkness will hide me and the light become night around me,"

> even the darkness will not be dark to you; the
> night will shine like the day, for darkness is
> as light to you.

No matter where I went or what I did, I heard a voice telling me, *He loves me, and He died for my sins.* This was the force that ultimately brought me back to Him. When I was just about seventeen years old, during one service, I heard my father preach. I was tired of running from God. I was like the prodigal son in the pig's pen, finally coming to my senses. I had tried everything that this world had to offer, and it all left me very miserable. At the end of the service, I raised my hand during the altar call and asked Jesus back into my life. At that moment, it felt like a huge weight was lifted off my shoulders—like scales were removed from my eyes. For the first time in a very long time, I felt free. I remember the joy that came over me. I felt peace—God's peace—that those who know Jesus have in their lives.

On that day, the process of restoration began. So much damage was done in my life that I needed the restoring power of God to be demonstrated in me. A lot of people didn't believe that I was truly saved that day; they thought it was all a show. But I knew that on that Sunday morning, my heart was desperately sincere. I came back home.

For the next several years of my life, I got involved, helping in any way that I could at church. God slowly worked in my heart, molding and making the man that He wanted me to be. I even spent four months in a faith-based men's recovery home. There I learned a lot about being a disciple, and I got to deal with a lot of personal issues that I battled. When I got out, I continued to grow at my home church. In time, I married my high school sweetheart, Sabrina. We immediately started a family, and life went on.

As time passed, that fresh flame that I carried when I rededicated my life to Christ was nearly extinguished. I pretty much went to church with no desire to really do anything for God. I had my own plans, none really involving God. Don't get me wrong—I loved Christ, but my future wasn't fully surrendered to His leading. I was consumed with my agenda instead of God's plan. Many times, we can become so preoccupied or burdened by life that we forget the one who gave us life and the purpose for which He gave it. That's where I was. But God wasn't finished with me yet.

Do you remember the pastor I talked about in the beginning of this chapter—the one who called me out for prayer when I was a young teen? Well, about a decade later, he was invited again to my father's church. During this time, I had already been married for a few years and had three kids of my own.

After a great sermon, the pastor was just about to hand the microphone back to my father when he looked around the audience like he did a decade earlier. He looked me right in my eye and called my wife and me up to the front for prayer. He started telling me things like he was reading my mail. God knew—He always does. Every word the pastor told me was like an arrow on a bull's-eye.

The pastor said, "You feel like you have lost the anointing." That was exactly how I felt. I was moving on with my life. I thought the dreams of preaching that I had as a young boy and a young man were over, but God had different plans. The pastor went on to say, "God is giving you a greater anointing, and He is going to raise you up for His glory!"

With every word the pastor proclaimed over me, a dead man came back to life. The dreams that I thought were over were just beginning. Prayers were answered. I received a divine download from heaven. God restored me, and this time, I didn't resist the Holy Spirit. The author of the book of Hebrews puts my whole life into perceptive with this verse: "Let us fix our eyes on Jesus, the author and perfecter of our faith, who for the joy set before him endured the cross, scorning its shame, and sat down at the right hand of the throne of God" (Hebrews 12:2).

During countless times, I find that Jesus is the author of my life story. He works relentlessly behind the scenes, protecting me, shielding me, and keeping me by His unwavering power. He knew what was up ahead and orchestrated the doors I would face—the doors He would open and the doors He would close. Ironically, a few years after that spoken word and countless confirmation from others, my wife and I were ordained to pastor in front of our beautiful mother church in Norwalk, California.

That evening, I was called to preach in front of hundreds of people. This was the fruit of my father's prayers, my beloved mother's prayers, and the intercession of my beautiful wife.

Conclusion

Years have passed since that fateful day of my ordination. The more that I serve God, the more I see Christ's handiwork on the canvas of my life. There are times when I wonder why God chose me. The only reason I can find is "amazing grace." This is the strength that pushes me to believe when my circumstances tell me not to. My story is proof that the worst prodigal church kids are no match for Christ. God can save the most unlikely and use them for His kingdom. This is not because I'm special, because I'm a pastor's kid, or anything like that. My return to Christ rests solely on Him. When I'm reminded of all that He has done already, I'm forced to believe that He isn't finished.

Broken Hearts, Hurting Parents

> Then Jacob tore his clothes, put on sackcloth and
> mourned for his son many days. All his sons and
> daughters came to comfort him, but he refused to be
> comforted. "No," he said, "in mourning will I go down to
> the grave to my son." So his father wept
> for him. Genesis 37:34-35

HAVE YOU EVER MADE A complete stranger cry the first time you met them? Hopefully not—but with one innocuous question, I did. It all happened at my local bank. When I was called up to the teller window, the banker quickly noticed that I was making a deposit for my church. She began to say that her husband was a minister in the city next to ours. She talked proudly about him and about how her daughter was going to start her first semester at a prominent Christian university in southern California. The conversion went well until I asked, "So, do you have any more kids?"

A long pause preceded the teller's words. Then she somberly replied, "Yeah, I have a son."

I should've been aware of her tone and read her facial expressions more accurately, but I didn't. I continued my insensitive interrogation with one more question, and this one broke the piñata. "So, where does he live?"

With those five short words, I made this woman cry. Quickly, all eyes turned in our direction. With the whole bank listening to our conversation, she quickly wiped her eyes and uttered the words, "I don't know where he is."

Then she cried some more. Promptly, one of her coworkers came to her aid, putting her hands on the teller's shoulder and asking her, "Is everything okay here?"

The teller said, "Yeah it's just my son." After that, I remained silent until she was done with my deposit.

It was time to leave, but I didn't want to leave the woman shattered. Before I left her window, I said, "I was a prodigal, too, but I came back to God." That was all I could say. It was the only bit of hope that I could offer. With that, she nodded her head in gratitude, and I exited the building.

That story reveals the pain that many parents experience. In comparison to all the possible things that can happen to our children (with the exception of death), the pain brought by a prodigal child exceeds them all. Nothing breaks the heart of a parent more than having his or her kid leave God.

Thousands of parents across the world have felt the sting that prodigals bring. No time zone or terrain is exempt. Prodigals saturate every race and culture. Across all denominational lines, from conservative Baptist to Pentecostal, we find prodigals. Since the beginning of time, prodigals have turned away from the laws of God and brought heartbreak to their parents.

Since I've been in church all my life, I've witnessed some of my closest friends that I grew up with leave God. These kids went to the same church and heard the same preaching. We sat next to each other during Sunday-school. We attended the same youth conventions. We shared the same teachers, pastors, programs, and curriculum.

And for a season, we all loved God. Then for some foolish reason or another, we all left God. My return to Christ is bittersweet for many of my friends' parents. They want their kids back, too—and rightfully so. Many are great parents. They taught their kids the difference between right and wrong. They trained their sons and daughters in the things of God—not just by word but also by deed. They did not merely speak the Word to their kids but showed the Word to their kids by their conduct. When I see these parents, their eyes tell me the heartbreaking story that their children are still far from God. Their feelings of sorrow cannot be hidden by their smiles and warm greetings. It's obvious they are hurting and in desperate need of hope.

Some are offered no hope from their children. No signal of return is given to heartbroken fathers. Their children's actions say, *I'm not coming home,* and their mouths say the same. There is no gasp of fresh air for the mother whose hope is nearly suffocated. Most have no regret, remorse, or repentance for what they have done or for what they are doing.

Occasionally, their parents tell me things like, "Please keep my son in your prayers," and "Can you give my son a call? He really liked you." When they walk away, my heart really goes out to them. They're asking me to pray for their kids, not some distant person who they met once. Their flesh and blood—their baby boy or little princess—are the ones they talk about.

Many parents think their child's departure is their fault. They feel it's a result of something that they did. Some carry guilt over something that they didn't do. All these negatives produce exactly what the enemy was scheming for. Thankfully, the Bible offers us hope during these dire circumstances—and sometimes from the least likely characters.

Jacob was the Old Testament patriarch who wrestled with an angel all night long and fearlessly wouldn't let go until God's messenger blessed him. The Bible records this encounter in Genesis 32:24. I always wondered why God allowed this to happen to Jacob in the middle of the night in the lonely eastern desert. Many believe it was because God wanted Jacob to stop running from his brother, Esau, whom he stole the firstborn's blessing from. Others say that it was the result of his past catching up with him—and Jacob certainly had a shady past. Still others say the name change from Jacob to Israel signified new beginnings in his life.

But if we look just a little deeper in the text, we find that God was preparing Jacob for his future. This incident was a divine event that was scheduled in God's calendar long before it occurred. God sees the beginning from the end. He's not just ten steps ahead of us. The fact of the matter is that He's infinitely ahead of us. That encounter with God's angel was preparation for a bigger fight—the struggle that all parents with prodigals face—the battle of hopeless heartbreak.

We all know that Jacob had twelve sons. But out of them, Joseph, was Jacob's favorite because he was born when Jacob was already up there in age. Unlike his brothers, Joseph was an obedient child, which made his brothers even more jealous of their little brother. The Bible states that Jacob made a well-ornamented robe full of many colors for Joseph (Genesis 37:3). It was not just any old robe that they wore during those days; it was elaborate, beautiful, and a symbol of Jacob's love for Joseph. This coat of many colors represented the special favor that Joseph had from his father.

Around the same time that Joseph was presented with the robe, he had a series of dreams that pointed to him being elevated above his whole family. Talk about being on top—Joseph had the dreams and coat of many colors. He was his father's right-hand man. There was just one little problem. Joseph's older brothers didn't like the idea of their kid brother running the show, and it definitely didn't sit well with them that their father Jacob favored Joseph more than them.

Was this a normal case of jealousy? No, Joseph's brothers almost killed him because of it. Fortunately, the eldest brother, Reuben, came to the scene before the other brothers' heartless scheme could be accomplished. But in spite of all that Reuben could do, Joseph was still sold as a slave to a group of Midianite merchants. To cover up what they did, the sons of Jacob killed a goat and drenched Joseph's richly-colored robe in the goat's blood.

> Then they got Joseph's robe, slaughtered a goat and dipped the robe in the blood. They took the ornamented robe back to their father and said, "We found this. Examine it to see whether it is your son's robe." He recognized it and said, "It is my son's robe! Some ferocious animal has devoured him. Joseph has surely been torn to pieces." (Genesis 37:31-33).

Although this is a sad story of Jacob losing his precious son, Joseph, the story is far from finished. We know that for the following seventeen years, Jacob thought his son was dead. Joseph went from place to place—from Potiphar's house, to prison, to then become the second-in-command of all Egypt. As we read the account in Genesis, we see that God purposely placed Joseph exactly where He wanted him for something greater than his father could ever imagine. It goes to show that some dreams seem like a nightmare at times. From Jacob and Joseph's life, you can learn some great lessons to encourage you through the heartbreak that prodigals bring.

What you have done is not a waste. The first area I want to touch on is one that makes many parents discouraged. They think that their spiritual investment was all a waste. Many feel like all their godly training, time, money, and prayers for their kids were for nothing. The enemy comes with the bloody robes like Joseph's brothers came to Jacob with Joseph's. The adversary taunts parents with the bloody robes, saying, "Look at all you did for him. It was all a waste—look at what he is doing now!"

Joseph's coat represented all of Jacob's hard work. The Bible says that Jacob made the robe with his own hands. He fashioned it, intricately knitting each color into the next. The garment was not only a symbol of his favor, but also a symbol of a parent's investment into his or her child.

This is a picture of many great parents in the body of Christ. These parents have done all they know to do only to have their kids leave God during high school or college. It's probably true that your kids probably aren't in the same circumstances as Joseph, who was forced to go to Egypt. But your kids might have gone to Egypt by their own choice—figuratively speaking, of course. That still doesn't nullify your investment into them. One verse that comes to mind regarding the subject of parental investment is found in Proverbs 22:6: "Train a child in the way he should go, and when he is old he will not turn from it." In this powerful promise are three things we can all glean from.

1. "Train a child" means to invest in her. Spend time, energy, and money to equip her for her dreams and destiny in Christ. My parents did this for me by placing me in a Christian school. My father modeled what it means to be a godly father, and my mother showing me what it means to trust entirely in God. They invested money, time, and prayer into my future, and now I am doing the very same things with my four kids.

2. "When they are old, they will not turn from it." Godly investment into our children will yield dividends. Some are apparent without delay; others might be seen in the long run. Reaping the benefits of your labor and risk is a given. God is still going to do what He promised to do.

3. The in-between season is a subject which we have to read in between the lines of this verse. This is the part that confuses everyone. The in-between can be looked upon as the time when things are not going the way that they were supposed to for godly parents. It's the waiting and worrying process. In my life, many (if not all) the people

I grew up with in church have left God at some point. I can only remember a small handful of my high school classmates who didn't abandon the faith.

My in-between season lasted about four years. These are four years I wish I could take back. Some people fight the Holy Spirit for months; others fight Him for years. We find that Jacob's in-between season for Joseph was seventeen full years. No matter how long you wait, know that your parental prayers are not wasted. Parents die, but their investment into their children's futures are always noticed in heaven and will touch their sons and daughters on earth long after their parents are gone.

Interestingly, Jacob's investment in Joseph was recognized in every place God sent Joseph. We see it in Potiphar's house, when Joseph ran away from temptation. We see it when he was locked in a cold prison cell and when he became a prince in Egypt. We even see it after his father, Jacob, died.

God is working behind the scenes. When Jacob thought his son was dead, God worked undercover in the life of Joseph. God is always at work, and many times in my life, He placed me in circumstances where I was almost forced to run to Him. In many instances, I didn't even know that it was His doing. This is very common in lives of prodigals. God allows certain things to happen—not because He is trying to harm a child, but because He's answering a prayer. For example, a prodigal may lose her job, have her boyfriend break up with her, or have a terrible nightmare about the rapture. Rude awakenings are sometimes great awakenings—especially in the lives of young people. Christ knows exactly where to apply the pressure and how to get your attention. It's part of His purpose to get things the way He desires them to be.

As a parent, you might not see God working, but that's because God works behind the scenes. God works in that realm because He doesn't want any outside influence to hinder what He will do. Some parents try to deliver their kids out of everything that God tries to place their kids in. Their hearts are sincere, but their actions are doing their kids more harm than good. They pay their children's bills, bail them out of jail, let them live in total compromise in their house without any discipline, give them money and pretend it won't be used for drugs and alcohol . . . and the list goes on.

If this coddling behavior continues to go unchecked, these parents aren't going to see their kids come to God, because they are stopping what He's trying to do in the lives of their children. I'm not trying to say that you should hand your kids over to the dogs and let them fend for themselves. However, what I am saying is that you should let God do His thing. And when this happens, He's able to work on what you've prayed for.

To bring this all into perspective, let me tell you a very embarrassing story about myself. When I was about sixteen, I wasn't saved. One day, I got beat up pretty badly by an older guy while skateboarding with a friend. If I go into all the details, it's pretty sad—but I deserved it, if not more! I didn't tell my parents; they didn't have the slightest clue—but God knew. He allowed it. Prior to this, there were a couple of narrow brushes with being jumped by groups of guys. But I always seemed to get away unscathed. This time was different; my actions finally caught up with me. My head hurt, and my jaw was sore from the guy repeatedly punching me in the face.

When I look back today, I'm glad it happened, because it woke me up. I started considering my actions. The stuff I was involved in at the time opened the door for that to happen in my life. My willingness to take a deeper look at my life was also an answer to my parents' prayers. That day, God was working behind the scenes for my mother. She didn't see or know it, but God was working. I didn't give my life over to Christ that day, but it was the beginning of my journey back to the cross. I think I finally surrendered to God about a year later—too bad it had to come to that.

I pray that it doesn't have to come to something like that for your prodigal to come back to God. Whichever method God uses is going to be the right one for your child. We must trust that God knows our children better than us, and He loves them much more than we could ever imagine. That He doesn't desire to hurt them in any way but permits things to happen for His purpose to be accomplished. Remember, He's always at work—whether you notice it or not. He sees your prayers for your child. He sees your heartache and the tears that you cry. Nothing you have done is unnoticed—not a prayer or a tear.

Conclusion

When we look back at Jacob's story, we must consider that during the end of his life, Jacob finally saw the dreams of Joseph come to pass. These dreams probably meant much more to Jacob than Joseph ever imagined. For many years, Jacob was a brokenhearted father who thought his son was lost forever. However, the dream was far from finished. The story of Jacob and Joseph is a shocking reminder that some dreams that we think that are dead are still alive. Whether you've lost all hope or still believe your prodigal will come back to Christ, remember Jacob. His life gives us all reason to place our trust in God.

REGAINING HOPE

Be strong and take heart, all you who hope
in the Lord. Psalm 31:24

KEEPING HOPE ALIVE IS AN inward battle. That's why the psalmist said, "Be strong and take heart." Things that remain unchanged can wear a person down. Recently, a woman I have known for years abandoned her faith and family. It really hurt, because I saw her battle for her unsaved family for years. She sacrificed much to see them saved and for a long time—only to give it up for a bowl of beans. When I inquired about her change of heart, I came to find that she felt she had waited too long, and nothing changed. Simply said, she lost hope. I wonder what would have happened if she stuck it out. Sadly, we'll never know. I pray she comes back.

HOPE VS. HOPELESSNESS

Hope can simply be defined as the inspiration to persevere in tough times and the knowledge that circumstances will someday turn in our favor. *Hope* is a beautiful word. It's a word that pushes us beyond our limitations. Hope makes us strive when we are given no good reason to. It makes us continue in life's battles when we are tired and weary.

Hope compels us forward. Like fresh water to the thirsty soul is hope to the human spirit. It makes us hold on when life weighs us down. Hope drives us to press on during seasons of discouragement. It encourages us to go forward when we are tempted to drop out. It makes us believe that someday, maybe today, things are going to turn our way. If the purpose why Christ came to earth could be summed up in one word, it could be the word *hope.*

Conversely, *hopelessness* is an ugly word. It's a word that pushes people to the grave early. Hopelessness makes us unconscious to every voice of encouragement. It makes us weary and exhausted. It kills inspiration, and it robs the motivation that God desires for us to have. No doubt, hopelessness is God's biggest critic—a close kin of skepticism. It desires to push us backwards. Like decay to the bones is hopelessness to the human soul. It makes us let up, back up, and ultimately give up. Hopelessness makes us believe that things will only get worse. If the enemy's plan could be defined by one word, it would be the ugly word *hopelessness.*

Just like the body needs water to survive desert conditions, the soul needs hope to survive hopeless circumstances. Interestingly, water and hope are a lot alike; the two sustain us when we are drained. Both replenish us when we are empty. Water hydrates the body; hope hydrates the spirit. One satisfies the heart; another satisfies the thirsty. Both are vital to our survival. After three days without water, we die. After one day without hope, our dreams begin to die. Just like we can't live without water, we can't live without hope.

Take a good look at your heart and with all that is going on in your life at this moment with your prodigal. Where are you in regard to your levels of hope? To make this clearer, imagine that you're at your kitchen table with three glass cups in front of you. The first is overflowing with clear, cold drinking water; the next cup is half full; and the last glass is empty. The water in the first two glasses represents the hope we have in our hearts.

With that in mind, let's break these down. First off, the empty glass can be labeled as someone who has no hope whatsoever. Sure, he can fake it, and act like he has everything under control. But deep down inside his heart of hearts, he doesn't believe that God can do what His Word promises. He thinks God can only bring back prodigals for others but not for him. When you try to encourage the hopeless, some are quick to turn off and say things like, "You don't understand my situation. You don't know my child, and you don't know what they are involved in!" Their focus is one-sided; all they see is the negative, demeaning, and discouraging. When God sends things to encourage them, their hopelessness blinds them from seeing it.

Secondly, we find the glass that is half-empty. This reveals the kind of people who have hope—but it's a mediocre hope. This glass is defined by halfheartedness and a lukewarm spirit. These people use the word *but* a lot in saying things like, "I've always believed God can bring back my son, but . . ." and "I know my daughter will return, but . . ." and the infamous "I'm praying and hoping, but . . ." They let doubt scribble a question mark on the promises of God.

Because we are real, we all have thoughts of doubt that bombard our minds. But people stuck in this place occasionally invite Mr. Doubt, Mrs. Discouragement, and their little rugrat, Despair, over for dinner. Instead of immediately rebuking the lies of the enemy for what they are, they casually entertain them. These people let doubt move into their minds and hearts like an unwanted intruder moving into a guest room. This is why they find themselves on a perpetual see-saw—up and down—because they are entertaining the wrong voices instead of God's voice.

And finally, the full glass represents people who take God at His Word. They firmly stand on the promises of God—not because their prodigal doesn't give them problems or because they don't face real-life trials, but because they choose to focus on what God's doing on their behalf, even if it's small. They're determined to stand on promises of God instead of sinking into their problems. When the enemy sends fiery darts of discouragement and unbelief, they quickly speak words of faith to extinguish them. They won't take no for an answer, knowing that regardless of how bad things may look right now, God is moving in their situation.

So where do you find yourself in this three-glass analogy? Are you the empty cup, completely hopeless? Or do you fall in the halfhearted category, giving way to doubt, fear, and failure? Hopefully we are full of hope—not only full, but overflowing! The apostle Paul said, "May the God of hope fill you with all joy and peace as you trust in him, so that you may overflow with hope by the power of the Holy Spirit" (Romans 15:3).

God doesn't just want our lives to be full of hope; He desires our lives to be overflowing with it! I love how Paul describes God in this text as "the God of hope." That's the God we serve. We don't serve the God of hopelessness or the God of discouragement and definitely not the God of despair. We answer to the Creator of the entire universe, who beams with enough hope to fill every heart that has ever walked on earth. He not only wants to fill our hearts half full or to the top, but He also has enough so we all can overflow with hope in our lives! How do we get there? And is it also possible to regain hope that has been lost? The good news is that the answer is yes!

The first step in regaining our hope is realigning ourselves with God's Word. The Bible says, "For everything that was written in the past was written to teach us, so that through endurance and the encouragement of the Scriptures we might have hope" (Romans 15:4). In that verse, we find that everything written in the Bible was written to impart hope, encouragement, and endurance for God's people. But the Bible wasn't just written to encourage us; it was also written to change us—to realign our thinking, make the crooked straight, make the wrong right, and expose the lies of the enemy for the truth found in Christ. Just like a car needs to be realigned from time to time, our minds and hearts need to be realigned with the Scriptures daily if we are going to experience victory.

Trials are a lot like potholes on the road; they can knock us out of spiritual alignment. Potholes make our thought life veer to the left and to the right when God's Word has called us to go straight ahead. For example, there is a mother reading this right now who has let thoughts of doubt penetrate her heart that her lost son will never come back to Christ. Those thoughts of doubt and discouragement make her swerve from faith in his return to failure that he'll ever return. Those are potholes that want to twist our focus from the promises of God to believing the lie that God can't do what His Word says he can do. Is God's Word realigning your thinking when the potholes of discouragement and despair hit? It should be.

The Word of God boldly declares, "For the word of God is living and active. Sharper than any double-edged sword, it penetrates even to dividing soul and spirit, joints and marrow; it judges the thoughts and attitudes of the heart" (Hebrews 4:12). We find here that the Word is breathing! Some see a dusty old book, but if they would take time to open it, they'd find that it's living, speaking, and powerful.

The Bible is not the all-time bestseller because the world wanted it to be. It's on top of the charts because it's alive.

Communist countries have banned its use; nevertheless, copies penetrate enemy lines. How did this come to be? It's alive. People went to the gallows, to wooden stakes, in front of firing squads, and laid their lives down for it—why? It's alive. The writer of Hebrews doesn't say the Bible's dead and dormant; he says it's alive and active. Applying this to our lives, if something is living and active, it has the power to affect what it comes into contact with. Let's examine what it does for us.

The Scripture aids us in regaining hope because it guides us. Recently, my family was vacationing in southern California in a place that I was totally unfamiliar with. As we were driving, I remembered that the new phone that we purchased had built-in navigation. So every time we got lost while driving, I would pull over and type in my desired location. Then in a matter of seconds, I was back on the road with step-by-step directions to our destination.

The Word in your heart is like a navigation system in a car. It guides us in which course to take and which thoughts to think. It tells our heart take a left here and swing a right up ahead, and when we fail, it recalculates our course so we can ultimately make it where God wants us. The apostle Paul wrote, "Finally, brothers, whatever is true, whatever is noble, whatever is right, whatever is pure, whatever is lovely, whatever is admirable—if anything is excellent or praiseworthy—think about such things" (Philippians 4:8).

Those are the types of thoughts the Scriptures will guide us to mediate on. Paul doesn't write, "Finally, friends, whatever is false, whatever is unfortunate, whatever is wrong, think about such things!" The Bible leads us to focus on things that will—sooner or later—bring us to victory, not on things that will burden us down to the floor.

The Word revives us. A great example of this is found when we hear preaching and teaching at our local church, because they both revive us. For example, there have been times in our lives when we are discouraged and tempted to quit. In our state of circumstances, we go to church and sit through an anointed sermon that stirs us to go forward. Like a laser beam, the message points directly to our need. It seems like the minister hired a private investigator to gather information about us. God knew exactly what we needed and supplied it.

The Word will edify us. The word *edify* is rooted with the word *edifice* or *building*. A good word picture for *edifice* would be a medieval castle or cathedral—something built high and strong. That's what Scripture does—it builds us. On the other hand, the enemy wants to destroy all that God desires to build in our lives. A majority of all the attacks of the enemy comes through questioning God's Word. When we question and doubt God's Word, the enemy begins to take a sledgehammer to all that Scripture is building in our lives.

When someone starts doubting the Bible, her hope crumbles, and the floodgates of destruction open. Years ago, I had a dear friend who wrestled with doubt in God's Word. He was gifted and at one time believed Scripture. You noticed that God had great things up ahead in his life. At one point, it seemed that he surrendered fully to God. The Lord was even using him to reach young people through music. But as time went on, he began to question the Bible, and things started to fall apart.

In the course of time, he left God, and the last I heard, he was still searching and very unhappy. I often think and pray for him. It was apparent that God had great things up ahead for him. But he let doubt hinder his hope, and as a result, his doubt demolished everything God desired to build. This story shows us the importance of taking God at his Word. When we do, God is able to build us for His glory, and when we don't, our world falls to pieces.

The second step in regaining hope is trusting in God. The writer of Proverbs put it best when he wrote, "Trust in the Lord with all your heart and lean not on your own understanding" (Proverbs 3:5). Trust is a prerequisite for hope for the simple reason that we cannot hope in something or someone we don't trust. This is also true in our relationship with the Lord; if we don't trust Him, our mistrust will hinder us from hoping in Him.

Distrust hampers hope; it blocks us from where God wants to take us. So why do people live in the bondage of mistrust toward God? Well, sadly, a person's perception of God was shaped by events, circumstances, and people. For example, there could have been someone he looked up to as a child who was a promise-breaker, never keeping her word. As a result, the young person becomes cynical and closed toward others who carried some sort of influence in his life. The young person carries this warped view of people to his relationship with Christ, never fully surrendering to trust God because of all the broken promises from others.

This mistrust affects many. There are women who can never trust men and men who can't trust women; there are kids who don't trust their parents, and parents who can't trust their kids. You get the point. They can't trust, because they live in ignorance to the fact of faith that God isn't like people! He isn't a liar, He isn't a promise-breaker, and He isn't out to hurt anyone. He doesn't forget. He treats all people equally. He doesn't play favorites, and He desires to bless all of us.

Look at what God's Word says on this subject: "God is not a man, that he should lie, nor a son of man, that he should change his mind. Does he speak and then not act? Does he promise and not fulfill?" (Numbers 23:19)

We see the obvious negatives of mistrust, so let's examine the benefits of trusting God. Trust allows us to experience freedom. Paul wrote in Galatians 5:1, "It is for freedom that Christ has set us free. Stand firm, then, and do not let yourselves be burdened again by a yoke of slavery." When we do not trust God, we are burdened with heavy weights of mistrust; but when we trust God, we stand in freedom.

Imagine being imprisoned and losing your freedom for a crime you didn't commit. The pain of being behind bars and isolated from your family and close friends would devastate anyone. But this is exactly what happens when we choose not to trust God; we lose our freedom, peace, and joy, because distrust imprisons us. When we fully trust the Lord with our hearts, that is when we experience true and lasting freedom.

Another benefit of trusting God is that we take burdens out of our hands and place them in God's hands. There are some things that we can only trust God to change in the life of a prodigal. Of course, we plan, work, invest, and fight, but there are times when you might come to the edge of the Red Sea, and all you can do is trust that God will open the raging waves before you. Trusting in Him takes the burdens from your shoulders; they're transferred to Christ. When this happens, God exchanges your burdens for His peace.

The final step to regaining hope is being aware that promises require patience. Theoretically speaking, every parent whose prodigal comes back to the Lord has a PhD in the subject of patience. This is because nothing is instantaneous, especially when it comes to prodigals coming back home. Some take months to come home, and others take years. At any rate, the homecoming was worth the wait! The example of these parents is one to follow—a model of patience which is the opposite of what we see in our world right now.

We are fully aware that we live in a "give it to me now" generation. From fast food to instant messaging, our society is consumed with immediate gratification. Technology has forever changed how we do things—principally when it comes to patience. We can take care of a lot with the push of a button. We can check our bank accounts, read the latest news, pay some bills, order a pizza, and download our favorite movie in the span of about five minutes—as opposed to fifteen years ago, when all this would take the whole day.

We may wonder why many times, our unanswered requests take so much time. Believe me, it's not that God can't be "high-speed" or that He's behind on the latest technological advances. God has answered some of my prayers very quickly; others I'm still waiting for. We can safely conclude that He's just too advanced to give us things too soon and too smart to be high-speed. Many people want God to work like a microwave when He cooks more like a Crock-Pot. Ironically, the Bible says this in regards to heaven's clock, "One day is like a thousand years and thousand years are like one day" (2 Peter 3:8).

God is divinely patient beyond our understanding, but He also desires and requires that His children wait patiently for His promises. Moreover, Peter wrote, "The Lord is not slow in keeping his promise, as some understand slowness. He is patient with you, not wanting anyone to perish, but everyone to come to repentance" (2 Peter 3:9, NIV).

The overall context of this Scripture pertains to the second coming of our Savior, but in this verse, we also see a great example of how the timing of heaven works. Peter wrote, "The Lord is not slow in keeping His promise." Do we disagree with the chief apostle? Probably so—for the simple reason that God's timing isn't the same as ours.

For the most part, God doesn't move when we hope. His agenda usually isn't synced with ours. As a result, some quit believing in the promises of God and miss the blessings that God had in store for their lives. Our motto should be, "Before a big blessing is a huge testing, and when we're hardest hit, that's when we must not quit!" In these seasons, God is testing and stretching our faith. These seasons are when He moves the most for us.

A word of caution—we can't let inactivity or silence allow us to retreat and waver in our hope. This is when we press on patiently for His promises. Don't let silence stop you. Silence doesn't mean that God's not involved, but it means that we have a chance to trust the Lord. This is where the foundation of hope comes into play.

Trusting in the timing of God is hard. Just ask Abraham, a man who had his promised son when he was nearly 100; or Moses, who was eighty when God finally called him; or Joseph, whose dream didn't come to pass until seventeen years after he had it. Many of those patriarchs waited, and God at times was silent. Their lives and the example of others show us that when God promises something, it might take more than twenty-four hours to come to completion. Regardless, God is always worth the wait. It's never a waste to wait on the Lord—but giving up is.

Conclusion

God made the anchor of hope to help us through life's storms. Right now, I know that many of you reading this have lost all hope from the circumstance and failures of your life or from the things that your prodigals are involved in. I think that it's best to close this chapter with a prayer to reignite hope in our lives. Repeat this aloud:

Father, you are the God of hope. Right now, I ask that you forgive me of my hopelessness. Forgive me for focusing on my failures and shortcomings. Help me to also forgive myself for my mistakes. God, I give you my doubt; I give you my failures and my discouragement. Lord, I receive your forgiveness, and now I boldly pray that you would fill my heart with hope! God, let my cup overflow with it. Let me focus on my blessings, and let me hold on to all your promises for my prodigal. Don't let me quit when times are hard. Don't let me waver when I am discouraged, but let me stand by faith and continuously hope in you. All this I ask in Jesus' name. Amen.

REACHING YOUR PRODIGAL

Jesus looked at them and said, "With man this is
impossible, but with God all things are possible."
Matthew 19:26

HAVE YOU EVER FELT LIKE reaching your prodigal was
impossible? There are all kinds of people we can
simply classify as unreachable, but we must remember that
no one is impossible for God to reach—and He's going to
use us to do it.

I was recently visiting with my aunt. All her children left
God during their teenage years, including my cousin,
David. For years, he was in and out of prison, used drugs,
and even fell into the web of the occult. He was the kind
of person who you would never in your wildest dreams
expect to come back to Christ! Without his family even
knowing where he was, he attempted to kill himself, but
before he did, he heard the voice of Christ call out to him.
After this encounter, he was a changed man. My proud
aunt, Christine, told me that he was recently ordained to
preach and showed us a video of him delivering his first
sermon at his home church in Arizona. As I watched the
video, I was blown away by the power of God. Of all my

family members who left God, he was the one I thought was least likely to come back to the Lord!

Even my own mother was a prodigal. At seventeen years of age, she would drive around town, full of anger and with drugs in her blood. She gave people the impression of hopelessness. One particular day, a local church was having an outreach event. Several of the volunteers saw my mother jump out of a car with a baseball bat in hand and all kinds of profanity coming from her mouth, loaded on drugs and yelling at the top of her lungs that Christianity doesn't work for anybody. One woman present that day told my mother later that she thought to herself, *Barbara is past the place of repentance.*

That misconception is exactly what I want to clear up. I really think that some parents and leaders are doing all the right things, but they feel like they're not because of the results they see.

That reminds me of the story of Zachariah and his wife, Elizabeth. The Bible notes that they were both blameless. They were faithful. They did all the right things— praying, believing, and treating others right. Nevertheless, Elizabeth was barren (Luke 1:6-7). In the Jewish culture at the time, this was a very shameful thing. It suggested sin and God's disapproval in a woman's life. This is reasonable cause to believe that she and her husband felt unnoticed and forgotten by God.

Do you share any common ground with Zechariah and Elizabeth? Have you ever wondered why things don't seem to add up? Maybe you have reached out to prodigal friends, and they still haven't returned to God. Or perhaps you did everything a good Christian parent has to do, and your kids still left God. Luke makes it clear that Elizabeth and Zechariah did everything that they were required to do, but their circumstance suggested that they hadn't. However, their story is far from over. The Bible says, "Do not be afraid, Zechariah; your prayer has been heard. Your wife Elizabeth will bear you a son, and you are to give him the name John" (Luke 1:13).

Elizabeth and Zechariah were well along in years; newlywed hopes of starting a family had evaporated with their age. But their prayer hadn't evaporated in heaven. It had finally come to pass on earth. This is a moving example of God keeping a good record and rewarding us in His time. If you feel like you're taking the wrong steps in reaching your prodigal because of the situation you're in—or he or she is in—don't. Take a good look at these next four points; they might reveal that you're on the right track after all. These are the things that God used to bring me back, and they are tools that He is going to use to reach your prodigal also.

Hold On to Your Convictions

When I was running from God, my Christian friends, leaders, and parents didn't let go of their godly convictions. I would have appreciated if they had watered down their rules a bit so I wouldn't feel so guilty, but they didn't! In hindsight, I wouldn't have come back if they did. Conviction is needed, because it's like a marker in a race; it's something that we can align ourselves with. Conviction gives us a standard to follow; it shows when we're out of line and need to reposition ourselves. My parents' conviction showed me my need for repentance. At the time, I didn't want to see or hear that, but deep inside, I knew I needed to change. My parents and leaders were able to accomplish this by giving me a pattern of godly convictions from these two areas:

- Their godly example—the importance of setting a Godly example cannot be understated, because if we are preaching one thing at church and living another way at home, it's a sure ticket for tragedy. We carry around invisible pulpits wherever we go, and prodigals are taking some good notes of who we are on the field and off. With that in mind, we should apply the words that the apostle Paul spoke to Timothy: "Watch your life and doctrine closely. Persevere in them, because if you do, you will save both yourself and your hearers" (1 Timothy 4:16).

- Faithfulness time and time again—when a person sets an example of faithfulness to God's Word, it creates a concrete pattern that younger people fully recognize. And as time goes on, it hardens; it becomes more visible. The faithfulness of my parents and leaders that I saw as I grew up was a testimony to what they claimed about Christ. It

Danny Casas Jr.

showed me that what they believed carried weight in their lives. Their faithfulness was evidence to me of God's faithfulness. And in time, this was a major influence in my return.

There are many things that want to water down your godly convictions, but those who keep them pass on an outlet of escape from the shackles of sin to their prodigal. Godly conviction is a must; without it, we'll be completely ineffective in reaching our children.

Keep Communication Alive

Never underestimate what a simple phone call or text message can do in the life of a prodigal. A word of encouragement can go a long way in touching him or her with the love of Christ. Interestingly, one of the major dynamics that you'll find in all prodigals that come back to Christ is relational ties. This is the connection of communication that they have between their parents, friends, and leaders. If this bridge is broken, the possibility of the prodigal returning decreases. These next points are critical in keeping the communication alive.

- We must remember to practice the lost art of listening. Many prodigals just want to be heard by their parents and leaders. Limit the interruptions; don't cut them off. A listening ear communicates the love of God more than 100 sermons— especially for a prodigal who has heard just about every sermon imaginable.

- Give your child your undivided attention, because young people can spot a counterfeit listener faster than a banker can recognize a phony $20 bill. Don't waste your time with halfhearted listening. It will just make matters worse.

- Pray for the right things to say. Saying something that the Holy Spirit didn't want you to say can really hinder or even destroy communication between you and your loved one. Our words can bring life or death, so we must let God lead us in this area.

Even if your child doesn't response to your phone calls, letters, and text messages, don't think that what you're doing doesn't matter, because even if it's not outwardly expressed by him or her, what you say matters immensely. Many times, your child doesn't want you to know that, because he or she is running from God. Also remember that your communication with our heavenly Father can still touch your child. As you communicate to God on his or her behalf, God in return communicates to them on your behalf. This action leads us to our next area in reaching prodigal children.

SPIRITUAL PERSEVERANCE

Pastor Jim Cymbala tells a poignant story about his sixteen-year-old prodigal daughter, Chrissy, in his book, *Fresh Wind, Fresh Fire.* Chrissy was gone, and he had no clue where she was. For months, he struggled to compose himself when he preached to his congregation because of his beloved daughter's departure. On one winter Tuesday night, as Pastor Cymbala prayed with his church, he received a note from a young woman who felt led to pray for Chrissy. Although he hesitated at first, he felt that something of it ringed true. After telling the church his dire situation, he describes that the atmosphere of the prayer meeting shifted into that of a "labor room." On the next Thursday morning, Chrissy came home!

Ironically, Cymbala writes of an interesting question that his daughter asked him that fateful morning at their family kitchen table upon her return: "Daddy, tell me the truth—who was praying for me Tuesday night?" He continues, "I looked into her bloodshot eyes, and once again I recognized the daughter we had raised."[3]

This story attests to the power of prayer. Have you ever noticed that when we start talking about faith, intercessory prayer, praise, and fasting, a lot of people start getting very uncomfortable? The enemy laughs in victory when this happens. Spiritual perseverance isn't easy. As a pastor, it pushes me out of my comfort zone. Every time I set my mind and heart to seek the Lord, things just seem to happen.

Is it just me, or can you relate? For example, you may set time aside to pray, and the phone begins to ring off the hook. You may plan to fast a day for your prodigal when your coworker surprises you with lunch! Is it just

[3]   Jim Cymbala. *Fresh Wind, Fresh Fire*. Grand Rapids: Zondervan, 1997.

a harmless coincidence or something much deeper and darker working behind the scenes to extinguish any fresh spiritual flames that are begging to ignite? The apostle Paul put it like this: "For our struggle is not against flesh and blood, but against the rulers, against the authorities, against the powers of this dark world and against the spiritual forces of evil in the heavenly realms" (Ephesians 6:12).

In this text, we are given a sneak peek into the unseen world. This dark realm is always in opposition to God's law. The enemy is real and wants us unconscious of its existence. Many times, people fail to consider the spiritual when dealing with the natural. Some fight with all their strength in the natural and miss the fact that "our battle is not against flesh and blood."

Sadly, some people believe in Jesus and that prayer works, but they still fail to pray. We must always remind ourselves that the doors to heaven's resources are unlocked by a golden key called prayer. Prayer is our conduit to the kingdom. It has the power to change any atmosphere, break any bond, and deliver even the worst of prodigals. Conversely, a prayerless life builds a road block—a great divide between us and God. Prayerlessness robs us of all that Christ desires to bestow upon us. Remember that nothing of true significance transpires when there is an absence of spiritual perseverance.

I suggest that if you really want to see God move in the life of your child, you'll apply the following traits that are evident in every prayer warrior that I know. They are:

- *Fervent prayer* It isn't a halfhearted, wishy-washy request; they pray to get God's attention. You hear desperation, intensity, and sincerity in the words that they pour from their hearts before the Lord.

- *Discipline* They schedule special time to be alone with the Lord, and they don't let anything or anyone disrupt their meeting. Usually early in the morning or when most are asleep, they beseech God on behalf of their children.

- *Praying without ceasing* As they go throughout their day, prayer and praise are on their lips and in their hearts. Continually, they let their petitions come before the Lord.

- *Praying until something happens* Elijah earnestly prayed for rain but didn't see any visible signs that rain was coming until his servant came to him the seventh time (1 Kings 18:44). This is the promise that people of prayer hold fast to. They don't let up until they've touched heaven.

These are the things that you'll find in every person who has breakthroughs in his or her prayers. The enemy will do anything to stop us from doing these things. The enemy will let us read, talk, and even think about prayer, but when we actually start doing it, the enemy hates it and will try to stop it! Right now, I challenge you to put the book down and pray for your prodigal until you feel a peace in your heart about him or her.

GIVE YOUR CHILD A SECOND CHANCE

We know from experience that a second opportunity is priceless. But what does a second chance mean to a prodigal? When I was backslidden, I embarrassed my parents badly. But when I came back to the Lord, my parents forgave me. They gave me a second chance to prove myself. Now I know that they didn't have to. I also know that if they didn't forgive me, there is a huge possibility that I would've gone back out to the world. I am very thankful that my dad and mom were willing to give me a second chance. It meant so much to me.

Some people aren't as fortunate. They make a big mistake, and when they attempt to make their way back home, the doors are locked. Forgiveness isn't granted, and grace is forgotten. Many forget that harboring a grudge against those who have let us down will demolish the process of restoration, because forgiveness is essential for this to work.

If we refer back to the life of the prodigal son, we notice a powerful picture of second chances. The response of his father upon his return easily could have been very different. The father could have ranted, raved, and rebuked, but instead, he restored, rejoiced, and received. As a result of this profound demonstration of grace, the father received a backlash from his eldest son. At times, this could be the same attitude of some at church. Luke 15:28-30 says:

> The older brother became angry and refused to go in. So his father went out and pleaded with him. But he answered his father, 'Look! All these years I've been slaving for you and never disobeyed your orders. Yet you never gave me even a young goat so I could celebrate with my friends. But when this son of yours who has squandered your property with prostitutes comes home, you kill the fattened calf for him!

The older son gave his gracious father a hard time because his kid brother was welcomed back without having to make restitution for his crimes. He couldn't even celebrate that his brother wasn't dead. Instead of having joy because of his little brother's return, he started complaining and scolding his dad because he was excited that his lost son came home. This reveals a self-righteous spirit, which we can learn a great deal from.

- Self-righteousness makes us numb to what others are feeling. The elder son could not have cared less about the joy his father experienced on the return of his younger son. All that he could see was a foolish old man letting his wayward son off the hook.

- Self-righteous people look at others with a critical spirit instead of seeing a person who desperately needs their forgiveness. In a sense, a self-righteous spirit wants prodigals to stay in a critical condition. This spirit always looks at people in a stereotypical manner and treats them like they can never change.

A second chance sometimes is all that a prodigal needs. When someone grants a second chance to another, he grants that person grace. Without a second chance, the possibility of a prodigal returning is zero. Although it's easy to build walls around our hearts, sometimes we are pushed to take a risk with people.

Some are trapped by the fear of what others will say. Let me clarify that there are voices of truth that we honor and value, such as the voices of pastors, teachers, and godly friends. But by the same token, we must be aware that the enemy uses people who do not walk in the Spirit. Their opinion must not be taken to heart. "The opinion of others can't control us. The fear of human opinion disables; trusting in God protects you from that" (Proverbs 29:25, MSG).

Instead of asking, "What will people think of me when they notice my son left church to live a life of sexual depravity?" or "What will their opinion be when they find out my daughter is involved in such-and-such?" the question that we should ask ourselves is, "What does God think?"

These are the problems that good followers of Christ are up against. The truth is that we live in a fallen world with fallen people who are closely connected to the lives of good believers. They are our friends, sons, daughters, sisters, and brothers. They are the people we love, and they are the people God has called us to love. If we don't help them, who will? If we don't support them, who will reach out to them? At times, the love of God requires us to roll up our sleeves and get a little dirty. Don't let the fear of what others are going to say stop you from giving your prodigal a second chance. He or she might need more than one.

CONCLUSION

Holding on to your conviction, open lines of communication, spiritual perseverance, and second chances are the key ingredients in reaching your prodigal. An absence of one can equal the absence of them all.

These acts were the pieces that were most influential in my return. God used people to reach out to, encourage, rebuke, and love me. People like my parents, youth leaders, and friends who loved Christ and also loved me. They were the hands and feet of Christ. They took the time to demonstrate the message that they so passionately professed. At times, I'm sure I discouraged them. Some may have been tempted to move on, but they didn't. They reached me more than they could imagine—and probably more than I showed them.

THE POWER OF OUR WORDS

A word spoken out of season can mar a
whole lifetime.

GREEK PROVERB

WE CAN'T UNDERESTIMATE THE POWER of our words in the everyday lives of our prodigals. Our words can drive them away from God or restore them back to God. They can be a bridge to restoration or the explosives to a child's only bridge of return. Words have the power to both encourage and dishearten. They can build or demolish. Words can direct and mislead. Some can bring life to new dreams; others can crush them. They can ignite us with passion, but if carelessly spoken, they can snuff out fresh flames.

Last Christmas, my family and I drove to my parents' house to fulfill our family tradition. The house is always full of grandchildren in diapers, movies, and holiday games. As you probably already know, food, football, and family always result in good times, but this last Christmas blessed my socks off. It was business as usual; we arrived at my dad's house early Christmas day. My agenda was simple—eat, nap, and then eat again—but God's plan for me that day was totally different. Everything went as planned until just about noon, when my dad sat next to me in the living room. We began our usual routine of talking about church.

But on this rainy Christmas day, the conversion turned in an untraveled direction. My dad started to talk about a series he was preaching at his church on the subject of blessing and cursing. He explained to me the biblical power of a curse and then expounded on the benefits of blessings. He had my attention; I was taking mental notes so I could preach about it on Sunday morning at my church. And when he finished, a sentence came out of his mouth that I will never forget. He asked, "Danny, can I speak a blessing over you?"

I replied, "Sure." So right there in his living room, in front of my wife and four kids, my dad began to declare blessings over his grown son.

Dad started by saying, "I am sorry for not spending more time with you when you were a kid." At the sound of those words, I broke. Tears streamed down my face—and his. With every sentence that he pronounced over me, I felt like he was laying a secure foundation. Each word he spoke was firmly connected like bricks with mortar. He was building something that was already in heaven's blueprints. With those powerful words, I was blessed.

My dad's message to me that afternoon forever changed my life. I know that I wouldn't be writing this book if I hadn't received those powerful words that cold winter day. His words to me were golden. And his words of blessing to me only amplifies the influence of that small member between our lips called the tongue. The ancient wise man, Solomon, said this: "The tongue has the power of life and death, and those who love it will eat its fruit" (Proverbs 18:21). That means we are going to have to eat all our words, whether good or bad, happy or sad. We will be liable for every syllable that comes off our tongues.

Jesus absolutely raised the bar when He said, "But I tell you that men will have to give account on the day of judgment for every careless word they have spoken. For by your words you will be acquitted, and by your words you will be condemned" (Matthew 12:36-37). Now that's a heavy-duty standard from Jesus that should govern what exits our mouth every day. If we are going to see God do His will in our lives, it's going to be directly connected to the words we speak over ourselves. Even in the lives of prodigals, there is a divine link between our words and their destiny.

The Tale of a Tongue

The more that we study the tongue, the more fascinating it becomes. For example, some doctors say that the tongue is the strongest muscle in the body. Another remarkable fact about the human tongue is that out of all the parts of our bodies, it's the one that heals the fastest. Furthermore, like the human heart, the tongue never stops working. Even when we sleep, the tongue works right along, pushing saliva into your throat. A good question we should ask ourselves is whether or not our tongues (which I use interchangeably with words) are working for or against us. The answer to that tough question is revealed by four critical components of communication.

THE WORDS WE USE

When you're angry or disappointed, do you tend to use hurtful and critical words toward the person who disappointed you? Do you use four-letter words when you're irritated or mad? Do you have a pessimistic speech pattern toward your prodigal? Do you say things like, "I knew that you'd grow up just like your father," "You are a disgrace to me and your mother," or "I wish you would get out of my life"? If you answered yes to any of these, God really wants to help you.

LACK OF WORDS

Lack of communication could be just as hurtful to your prodigal as hurtful words. Some people think that no words will really teach the person who hurt them a lesson when the silence just drives a deeper wedge in the relationship. Some of my family members have been offended by others only to retaliate by building walls of silence to get even. For years, they wouldn't visit, call, or even forgive the other person for his or her wrong. Many years were wasted by the silent treatment, and many relationships were devastated.

The Tone of Our Voice

Many people don't get into hot water because of what they say but how they say it. Imagine how many marriages could have been saved from divorce if a husband or wife just lowered the tone during an argument. Our tone reveals our level of self-control and our level of love for those we communicate with. A loud and overbearing tone reveals the heart's condition and expresses, *I don't care!*

Body Language

Although body language isn't related to the tongue in a literal sense, it's without doubt an extension of the tongue. Ugly faces, sharp movements with the arms, and quick neck jerks have a way of making people feel unwanted and unloved. Our body language can speak a thousand words, so a good question to ask yourself is, *What does my body communicate?* It's very important to openly take a look at these four areas in your life.

Words Set Things in Motion

In the creation account, we find that God spoke things into existence (Genesis 1). By His words, He created the heavens and the earth. From the great trees of the sequoias to the millions of minuscule jellyfish on the Atlantic coastline and every mountain, valley, and wasteland in between. Everything from the law of gravity to morality is a result of God speaking.

One very interesting story found in the book of Numbers is about a man named Balaam. He was known for speaking blessings and curses. Whoever he blessed would be blessed, and whoever he cursed would be cursed. Balak, the king of Moab, knew this. When trying to get the Israelites off his property, he promised a large sum of money for Balaam to curse the nation of Israel. The only problem was that God told Balaam that he couldn't curse the nation of Israel (Numbers 22:12). However, the princes of Moab wouldn't take no for an answer, and they continued pressing Balaam to curse Israel. Finally, God told Balaam to go down with the messengers to see King Balak. God specifically told Balaam not to say anything without His command (Numbers 22:20).

When Balaam went to see Balak, one of the most bizarre things in the entire Bible happened. Balaam's donkey came to a halt, so Balaam struck it with his stick. Without Balaam even knowing, the donkey's eyes were opened to the spirit realm, and a mighty angel was blocking their passage! The donkey was stuck in its tracks, so Balaam struck her harder until finally, the donkey turned her head and started conversing with her master. The Bible says, "Then the Lord opened the donkey's mouth, and she said to Balaam, 'What have I done to you to make you beat me these three times?'" (Numbers 22:28)

From this outrageous dialogue that sounds like a scene from a 1950s sitcom, two unusual questions beg to be answered. Why did God send an angel to block this loyal donkey? And why did He permit this donkey to talk?

I believe the answer is found in Numbers 22:32: "The angel of the Lord asked him, 'Why have you beaten your donkey these three times? I have come here to oppose you because your path is a reckless one before me.'"

Did you catch the phrase, "because your path is a reckless one before me"? The path God was talking to Balaam about was his *word path.* Balaam started to be influenced by the Moabites, who wanted him to curse the Israelites. God saw what was going on in Balaam's heart, and He sent His angel to quickly regulate Balaam's words! This is revealed in Numbers 22:35, when He said, "Go with the men, but speak only what I tell you."

God sent His angel and allowed the first recorded talking donkey in all of history because God wanted to make sure that Balaam wasn't going to say anything that wasn't in God's playbook! God knows the devastation that words can cause to others.

When we perform a careful evaluation of our speech, there may be some things that we say in general or even directly to others that God might send an angel to prevent us from saying. God may even open the lips of your most beloved household pet to tell you to "Zip it!" I'm not trying to be redundant—but words are powerful, and blessings and curses lie between the lips!

If you're like some people, you might need to relearn to speak. Of course, you know how to put nouns, verbs, and adjectives together, but you may need help placing the right nouns, verbs, and adjectives together at the right time and in the right manner. Many people have been handed down bad vernacular habits from their elders. They talk just like their mothers, brothers, and others who weren't the most positive people to follow, especially in relation to the tongue.

Gossip, negative attitudes, complaining, and even foul language are hard to drop when they are passed down to you. Even in the Christian community, transformation must occur. For some believers, everything has been sanctified except their tongues. Their wallets have transformed, they have "Honk if you love Jesus" bumper stickers on the back of their minivans, but their tongues are still the same. No change has happened, and they are still unsanctified!

How can change occur in the tongue? I believe that it's possible for people to change the way they speak, but it's going to take the power of the Holy Spirit for this to happen.

Good Communication Deposits

It feels good to make a significant deposit into your saving account. Withdrawing isn't as exciting, and a bank account in the red is downright frightening. This is even seen in the word realm. With our words, we deposit into and withdraw from the hearts and minds of those around us. As a result, some are overdrawn because of their words!

Look back on all the words you said this past week to your loved ones. Which type of word transactions did you make? Have you been critical and negative or uplifting and edifying? Do your words make people draw closer to you, or are they driving them away? The following are three types of good communication deposits that can be filled by the guidance of the Holy Spirit to bless those around us.

Speak the Truth in Love

When I was in my rebellious days, my parents talked to me about my poor decisions. They laid down the consequences of my choices, and wherever I went and whatever I did, I remembered the truth. They communicated clearly and succinctly what was required of them—and most importantly, of God. They communicated in a way that pushed me toward the right path—and always in love. Even when they disciplined me as a child, it was never done out of anger but motivated out of love.

Some people think that it's impossible to speak the truth in love. In reality, truth should always be motivated by love. An absence of truth reveals a shortage of love. The ancient cliché says, "It's not what we say but how we say it." I think it's safe to say that it's not what we say but how we say it that dictates how others will take it! Our tone and word choice offer a good gauge of our levels of love and maturity.

God knows that you have problems with your prodigal, and there are serious issues that must be dealt with in a proper and timely manner. I think some people find themselves imbalanced. They're either overly pessimistic, always saying the worst, or foolishly optimistic, always burying their heads in the sand and not speaking the truth. We should be cautiously optimistic, find out what's really going on, and speak the truth in love with those He has entrusted to our care. They'll respect you more if you tell them the truth, and speaking it to them in love will disarm all their defenses and allow you to deposit truth into their hearts.

Hear Your Prodigal Out

Many times, prodigals are involved in things that you would rather tune out because the severity of the sin. No one wants to hear that her kid who she raised the best she could turned down a dark path. But it is critical that you hear your child out, because if you don't, someone else will—and the point of view this person carries isn't going to be the same as yours.

When I look back at my life, I remember moments when I had to tell my dad what I was struggling with. I'm sure my shortcomings and mistakes hurt him and made him angry, but he heard me out. As a result, I was able to hear him out also. For example, I remember on one occasion, I had messed up big time. My father took me out and spent a Sunday night with me—just him and me. He listened to me that evening. He didn't have to say one word; just the fact that he listened communicated to me what I had to do.

Captivatingly, James wrote, "Everyone should be quick to listen, slow to speak and slow to become angry" (James 1:19). This statement goes against the grain of modern-day communication. Many desire to be the speaker; few are willing to be the listener. But if we are going to reach our unsaved loved ones with our words, we must first be willing to listen to their words. Here are a few of the many benefits of active listening:

- Listening communicates that you care. When someone listens to you, it shows that you matter to him. On the other hand, when a person chooses not to hear us out, it's much easier not to listen to her.

- Listening draws others to you. Those of us who are married chose our spouses because they listen attentively to us. Listening is like glue that connects us and forms such a great bond that we are willing to spend the rest of our lives with our spouses.

- Listening releases others. When a person is stressed out and hurting, he needs someone he can talk to. We have all had bad days, and sometimes we just need another person to tell it to. After we talk, we feel better because we just had to get it out into the open. When we bottle things up, the stress grows, and it leads to many harmful side effects. When we hear someone out—in this case, a prodigal—it works to disarm that person's defenses and restore the preponderance of your voice.

A listening ear is powerful. When we give someone our undivided attention, in a way, we give that person our whole heart. Listening communicates love and builds a two-way road. You'll be able to tell the person you listened to things that are only possible because you first heard him out. When a prodigal is listened to, she listens, too. Listening is a great communication deposit!

Encourage Your Prodigal

Encouragement is a huge deposit! It can be underestimated or downplayed. It pays high dividends to those who use it wisely. When I was a teen, I struggled a lot with low self-esteem, depression, and suicidal thoughts. I hated life. I really thought I had no future. All I saw were the things in front of me, and they weren't good. Thankfully, my mother always encouraged me. She always told me that God had a great plan for my life and that God was going to bless me if I gave Him my life. She always encouraged me to live for Christ. She told me that God would bless me with a beautiful wife and use me for His glory.

My mother was right. God has blessed me with a beautiful wife who deeply loves me and loves Christ. And yes, God is using me for His glory; I'm a pastor of a wonderful church. But what if my mother didn't encourage me? What if she let her problems stop her? She's a pastor's wife, and I'm sure the stress levels of her position were overwhelming.

But she would put herself aside and encouraged me. If she hadn't done this for me, things that were already going bad would've taken a devastating turn for the worst.

Parents, have you thought of how powerful a word of encouragement could be to your daughter who feels ugly or your son who struggles with low self-esteem? Maybe you came from a dysfunctional family and you were never encouraged. Maybe no one ever told you that you are beautiful or special. It's time to turn the tide and encourage your children, because you could be the only conduit of encouragement that they have.

Sadly, many suicide letters always seem to contain phrases like "Nobody cares, so I'm going kill myself!" It isn't true that nobody cared for the person; it may have been that those who cared failed to say that they did. Parent, pastor, teacher, husband, or wife, please don't fail to use one of the most powerful tools that God has given us to stop the agenda of the enemy. It's called encouragement. It kills discouragement and pushes the people we love to the places that God has called them to be.

Conclusion

Words out of a person mouth can't be seen, but the effects of them can. When you and I choose to speak what God says over our children, our words release the direction they are called to travel. The day that my father spoke his blessing over me on that promising Christmas morning made me believe that all the dreams that I had could actually become a reality. More importantly, his words released something that Abraham gave Isaac, Isaac gave Jacob, and Jacob gave his sons. It's called a blessing—a word spoken by faith from someone appointed by God upon a person they are anointed to lead. Have you spoken blessings over you prodigal? You should. Please declare blessings over your lost loved one. Repeat this aloud:

Heavenly Father, thank you for the freedom that you have given me through your Son, Jesus! Lord I confess that my words have gotten me in trouble many times. I have even said things that don't line up with your Word over my prodigal. I have even sinned by speaking words of fear over my child. But right now I want to speak blessings over my child by faith. By the power of the Holy Spirit, I boldly say that my child will serve you! By faith, I speak into existence that you would break each and every demonic stronghold in my child's life by the precious blood that you shed for us on the cross. Send forth your ministering angels to remind my child of your love, Lord. Right now, I speak protection over my child wherever she/he may be. I declare health over his/her body, provision to live in purity, confidence to walk into her/his destiny, and integrity to please you. All this I declare in the name of Jesus. Amen.

Building a Firm Foundation

The foundations were laid with large stones of
good quality. 1 Kings 7:10

IN THIS CHAPTER, WE WILL focus on what parents can
do to build a firm foundation before their kids leave the
house. When I was around nine years old, my father told me
a story that illustrates the importance of building things the
right way. I never forgot it. In many ways, this story can be
applied to the aspect of building a solid foundation in the
hearts of our children.

There was once a shady contractor who made a tragic
mistake. For many years, this man worked for his boss
but felt that he was not getting the wage he was worth. He
reasoned that he was working for peanuts. As time went
on, he began harboring resentment toward the man for
what he thought was unfair treatment and small wages.
Nevertheless, because of the shortage of job opportunities
in his community, he continued working for this boss.

Years passed by, and nothing of significance occurred—
no Christmas bonuses, no gas cards, no employee of the
month certificates—nothing. House after house, building
after building, project after project, it was more of the

same. Finally, he came to his breaking point, and this unseen employee became the bitter employee.

One day, the man's boss came to him and broke the news that he was retiring. The boss showed him the blueprints of the final project they would be working on. It was a magnificent house in the countryside. The disgruntled construction worker was quick to assume that it was going to be his boss's retirement home. He sarcastically thought, *This is my chance to get him back; I'll build a nice house for him to retire in!*

From the outset of the project, the man cut corners, did not following the blueprints, and overlooked possible safety hazards. The foundation wasn't level. Some walls were straight, and others weren't. Flooring wasn't installed properly, and kitchen cabinets where butchered. This shady contractor was on a mission—a mission that would leave him with a lifetime of regret.

Finally, the house was finished. The contractor called his boss to hand over the keys and receive his last paycheck. The old boss slowly got out of his dusty old truck with a check in his hand. As the dishonest employee handed over the keys, his boss smiled and said, "Son, you worked hard for me many years now. I never gave you what you deserved, so here's your last check, and here's the keys to this house—it's yours!"

The moral of this story is that we can't underestimate the importance of building things the right way—even our children. As parents, we are builders. You see a man playing with his daughter at the park; I see construction worker building her future. You observe a mother talking to her son at the family table during breakfast; I see a foundation being laid for the man he will someday become. *Builders* and *parents* are synonyms. Both words have the same meaning, because as parents, we are in a building project—our children are that project.

Parenting is not an easy task—especially in the day in which we live. There are costly mistakes that we can do without. There are temptations that want to divert us from being the parents God created us to be. There are voices that desire to hinder us from building our sons and daughters according to God's standard and God's blueprint. But regardless of the odds, negatives, and the pressing power of darkness in the world today, we can still tap into God's grace and find the strength we need to do things God's way. The cliché that states, "God won't give us more than we can handle" still rings true today. Although at times we feel that we can't bear the load, we have a precious Savior who is mindful of what we are facing (Psalm 8:4).

Before we begin laying the groundwork for building a firm foundation in the lives of our children, I must caution you that in no way am I saying that if you follow all these principles, your children will stay on the straight and narrow all their lives. We all wish it was that easy, but it isn't. The truth is you can do all the right things and still have children who do all the wrong things.

Years ago, my father took me out on one of his speaking engagements. After the service, we went out to eat with a man from the church. The young man started asking my father about how he did such a great job in raising his children to serve God. Little did he know that my father was facing a tremendous trial with one of my siblings at that time and that five years prior, I put my father's heart through the grinder.

My parents are great parents. But we must understand that great parents have prodigals, too. There's not some parenting formula that guarantees a 100 percent success rate. Sometimes people wrongly assume that if your children are rebellious, it's the result of not being a good parent, and if your children are good, it's the result of being a great parent. That couldn't be further from the truth, because the world's only perfect parent (God) had kids who both made a huge mistake that we still have to live with (Genesis 3:6).

I must also warn you that the last paragraph wasn't an excuse to be a lazy parent who doesn't teach his son and daughter the difference between right and wrong. But it should encourage us to build them the best we can, because I can say without a grain of doubt that if my parents didn't build a foundation of God's Word in my life, I would never have come back. They gave me something I couldn't escape, and it was truth. When I was a child, my parents built a solid foundation of truth that I could never break free from.

It All Starts with the Foundation

The foundation is the most critical part of any structure. It can be said that everything rises and falls on the quality of the foundation. This principle is seen in practically every facet of life. It's found in business, ministry, and even marriage. If there's not a solid foundation in these areas when the storms of life come, everything will come crumbling down. Jesus made this truth clear thousands of years ago when he said,

> The rain came down, the streams rose, and the winds blew and beat against that house; yet it did not fall, because it had its foundation on the rock. But everyone who hears these words of mine and does not put them into practice is like a foolish man who built his house on sand. The rain came down, the streams rose, and the winds blew and beat against that house, and it fell with a great crash. (Matthew 7:25-27)

In essence, Jesus was saying we should build our lives upon His words and live by them. Fathers and mothers are to walk in truth, live in truth, and stay in truth if they are to build a firm foundation for their children to glean from. The significance of foundations can't be overlooked or underestimated; our lives and the lives of our children depend on it.

Going to the Blueprints

Imagine how foolish it would be to start building a house without first looking at the blueprints. We know that walls would be in the wrong places, the right kind of materials wouldn't be chosen, and for the most part, the job site would be full of confusion. Nothing in the house would be right because no one would know where to start. Even the most capable people with years of experience and great carpentry skills, without the blueprints, are completely useless.

The same is true in raising children. If we aren't building according to God's Word, we are building the wrong way. In Scripture, every time God told someone to build something, He gave that person the exact details of how He wanted the project built. He left nothing to chance or to man's interpretation. God was always clear, and His purposes were precise.

Consider the life of Noah. When God came to Noah about making the ark, He didn't say, "So, Noah, I'm going to flood the earth in about 120 years. I was thinking about building a boat to save you and your family. Do you have any ideas?" No, God knew what had to be built and every element of how to do it. God told Noah, "This is how you are to build it" (Genesis 6:15). God didn't leave it up to Noah; He told Noah exactly what He wanted, down to the details.

We also got the blueprints and dimensions for how God wants us to build a sure foundation for our children. God's

Word is our compass; it is our guide and our navigation system. A powerful truth that Scripture reveals to us is that before we can build a foundation in the lives of our children, we must first have solid foundations in our lives. For the remainder of this chapter, we will look at three foundations that we need in our lives, beginning with foundation of personal integrity.

THE FOUNDATION OF PERSONAL INTEGRITY

"Do as I say and not as I do" is a popular saying nowadays. Sadly, this is what many parents are showing their children by their lifestyles and actions. Many parents tell their kids not to smoke, but they smoke. Others tell their children not to cheat, but they bamboozle others. Some say, "Don't lie," but they're habitual liars. Some say, "Don't disrespect authority," but they roast the leaders of the church at the dinner table right in front of the kids. We must remember the powerful proverb, "We can't give away what we don't have." If we are going to effectively build our kids, we must practice what we preach. Look at what the Bible says about this:

> You, then, who teach others, do you not teach yourself? You who preach against stealing, do you steal? You who say that people should not commit adultery, do you commit adultery? You who abhor idols, do you rob temples? You who brag about the law, do you dishonor God by breaking the law? (Romans 2:21-24)

The apostle Paul was telling us to take a good look at our lives and measure whether our words line up with our actions. These are some tough questions that we as parents need to ask ourselves because if we're not living on God's foundation, we most definitely won't build them in our children. Let's examine a few areas that are essential if we are to be the examples that our children need.

First off, we must ask ourselves the question, "Am I fully surrendered to the lordship of Christ?" This is critical, because our yielding to God touches each and every part of our lives. If we are completely surrendered, our attitudes will touch the lives of our children. The domino effect of being fully surrendered to God is a beautiful thing. When we leave everything at the feet of Jesus—when we empty ourselves of our pride, ambitions, and agendas—God is able to fill us with His presence, power, and perspective. When that occurs, we are capable of being the leaders God wants us to be.

Second, it's important to consider what our actions voice to our children. If I go to church once a year, I voice to my children that I really don't care about God. If the offering plate passes by and I drop an empty envelope into the basket, I voice to my son that he can care less about the kingdom of God. And if I bash and belittle my pastor on the drive home after church, I pass on the message to my family that they don't have to respect spiritual authority.

On the other hand, if I'm faithful to the house of God, I convey to my children the importance of placing God first. If my wife and I are faithful givers, we will produce hearts into our offspring that want to give to God also. And if I hold authority in high regard and demonstrate it by my respect and obedience to those who lead, that respect will be transferred to my kids. Our voices are our actions; our actions are our voices. The message that our voices send will lay the foundation of our kids' futures.

Third, there's always room for improvement. The incredible thing about being a Christian is that we have the ability to change. When we look at our hearts and the Holy Spirit shows us parts that need to change, do we listen to His leading? The Spirit might say to you, "Stop complaining in front of your kids, and start praising instead!" or "Take your son out, and just spend some time with him; show him my love." The Holy Spirit is the ultimate improver— always raising the bar and always pushing us to change for the better.

When we listen to the promptings from the Spirit for spiritual home improvement in our lives, our actions not only please God, but also open our eyes even wider, and His voice becomes clearer with every act of obedience. The foundation of personal integrity isn't the only foundation the Holy Spirit speaks to us about.

THE FOUNDATION OF ACCOUNTABILITY

Building a foundation of accountability in the lives of our kids is an effective way of teaching them to fear God and take responsibility for their actions. Accountability is essentially a system that is built on trust and openness between two people. When obedience is displayed, trust increases, and when disobedience occurs, consequences follow. The concept of accountability is found from cover to cover in the Word of God.

The story of Adam and Eve, God's first children on earth, gives us a great example of this concept and a paradigm to follow in holding our children accountable to God and to us. After Adam and Eve fell into sin, the Bible states that God came to garden and asked Adam, "Where are you?"(Genesis 3:9) Now that's a question we as parents should ask our children regularly. Knowing where they are is our responsibility as parents.

We should always be aware of our children's physical location and spiritual location, holding them accountable in both. But their spiritual location is what I want to focus on. This requires discernment, which basically means that you use your spiritual "nose" and are receptive to the voice of the Holy Spirit. To illustrate the importance of having spiritual discernment in our lives, an example from my adolescent days will drive this point home.

During my teenage years, I started doing some terrible things—and the Holy Spirit showed my mother! It was really amazing. For instance, if I was doing something that I shouldn't have, when I walked in the house, my mother gave me a look—almost like she smelled me! It was like I stepped in a big pile of dog dung. I'd try to tiptoe to my room, but she said in a very convicting tone, "We need to talk!" Then the cross-examination would begin

My mother's tactics have made me question whether or not she was in the FBI before I was born. She would start by saying, "Look into my eyes." Parents, after several minutes of torture like this, your children will be extremely convicted of the wrong they did. The eyes of your children will give you the scoop of what goes on in their lives (Matthew 6:22).

After probing my eyes for a few minutes, my mother began saying things like, "God's showed me what you did." Through this method, all my concepts of logical reasoning would melt away like a bag of crushed ice left on the sidewalk in the month of August. Half of my brain would say, *She wasn't there; how could she possibly know?* and the other half would say, *She knows. God showed her—you're busted!* Through those convicting cross-examinations, I learned some valuable lessons—and one is that that God sees everything, even the things done in secret. And also that building a relationship of accountability with your children is a powerful foundation that will lead them in a positive direction.

THE FOUNDATION OF QUALITY TIME

Strong foundations aren't built overnight. In a world of fast food, and quick diets, many would wish otherwise, but everything of true significance is built through time—even our children. With that in mind, there are a couple very important factors we must remember when building the foundation of time with our children. The first is simple—make time! One interesting note about Christ is that although He was extremely busy, He always made time to invest in children. "People were also bringing babies to Jesus to have him touch them. When the disciples saw this, they rebuked them. But Jesus called the children to him and said, 'Let the little children come to me, and do not hinder them, for the kingdom of God belongs to such as these'" (Luke 18:15-17).

Jesus took time out of His busy schedule to spend some quality time with these children. I'm sure that He was pressed for time. He had dead people to raise, blind eyes to open, and withered limbs to restore, but He stopped and made time for kids. That's a great example for us to follow. Nothing that we are busy doing today is as important as what Christ was doing during His three years of earthly ministry, yet He made time.

Another thing we learn from our Savior is not to kill time. We shouldn't waste it. The gospel of John records Jesus saying, "Let nothing be wasted" (John 6:12). There are many parasites that want to suck away our time with our kids. When dealing with this topic, a few obvious bloodsuckers come to mind, such as the Internet, TV, and plain old selfishness. But we must always remember that houses can be lost, cars can be stolen, and jobs can be terminated, but all these are replaceable. Time isn't like them; once it's lost, it's gone forever. It can't be replaced.

There's no time machine and no reversing the clock. We got one chance to make this hour count.

Not too long ago, a young man and I went out to eat at a local diner. After five minutes, a young family walked in and sat down near us. I quickly noticed that the husband was glued to his phone, and his wife was noticeably irritated by it. I don't blame her. Everyone on that side of the restaurant could hear her complaining to him, but all her protests fell on deaf ears. He wouldn't hang up. So she pulled her phone out and started doing the same. I kid you not—I saw two parents stuck to their phones for the rest of their dinner while their little girl sat there, all alone. Her parents where in a different world, and their faces showed it. The whole time they were there, I didn't hear her dad tell her one word.

It's really tragic that many parents are wasting valuable time on invaluable things. When I ask older parents for advice on parenting, 95 percent of the time, they give the same response. Their advice is, "Danny, your kids aren't always going to be little, so make sure you make every moment count." I can read in between the lines; they are tactfully telling me, "Don't blow this because you can't get it back." Jesus gave us the example of not being wasteful for good reason; He didn't want us to live with lives full of regret.

Conclusion

As parents, these foundations of personal integrity, accountability, and quality time are essential if we are going to build a firm foundation in our kids. We make a huge difference in our children's lives, training them in the ways of the Lord and building foundations for their future. Like the builder we talked about in the beginning of this chapter, we will get the keys to our children's hearts. We must keep the quality high because we'll have to live with the foundation we lay.

Fiery Darts of the Enemy

Sons are a heritage from the Lord, children a reward from him. Like arrows in the hands of a warrior are sons born in one's youth. Blessed is the man whose quiver is full of them. They will not be put to shame when they contend with their enemies in the gate. Psalm 127:3-5

One of the most powerful descriptions of parenting is found in Psalm 127. In this rare psalm that many attribute to Solomon, the psalmist likens a quiver of arrows to a household filled with children. In this text, parents are symbolic of warriors—unlikely characters, to say the least. The imagery that Solomon creates is of a battle in which the weapons for victory are held within the hands of parents. Just as a journeyman archer would point his arrows at the opposition, God has given us the responsibility to point our children toward the destination that honors Him. Parents are to aim their bows at the enemy to glorify His name and pass on a pattern of righteousness to the next generation.

This text contains two critical components that we must be mindful of, beginning with our need for God. The opening of the chapter says, "Unless the Lord builds the house, its builders labor in vain" (Psalm 127:1). This shows parents their desperate need for God. We need the direction and leading of the Holy Spirit to be effective as the builders and watchmen of our children. Our ears must be open to God's voice and our eyes watchful for His leading. If the Lord is not thoroughly involved in us and through us, we will succumb to defeat.

Second, parenting is spiritual. This is an aspect that some parents fail to recognize. Whether you're aware of it or not, we are engaged in an unseen battle against the principalities and powers of a nefarious kingdom whose chief leader is Satan (Ephesians 6:12). His agenda is to destroy everyone and anything that opposes him, including our children, because they pose a threat to his purpose. Although we point our kids in a direction opposite of his, he has a counterattack aimed at destroying them. The enemy of souls and his diabolical minions are relentless in their efforts to bring down our children.

All throughout history, we can see an invisible force plotting to destroy the next generation of the Lord's children and thereby hinder God's plan for mankind. For example, in the Old Testament, Pharaoh commanded that all the Hebrew boys born be killed (Exodus 1:16). Then in the New Testament, right before the birth of Christ, after King Herod heard that he was outwitted by Magi, ordered that all boys under the age of two be killed (Matthew 2:16).

Even today, the hideous plot continues. The unseen battle rages, and after all these centuries, the enemy still has its weapons aimed at the hearts of our children. The agenda is the same as it was in times past, but the battle is more complex. As parents, we can't afford to put our guard down. The apostle Peter gave us words to live by when he said, "Be self-controlled and alert. Your enemy the devil prowls around like a roaring lion looking for someone to devour" (1 Peter 5:8).

Now more than ever, parents must be wary when it comes to the arsenal of fiery darts the enemy shoots at our sons and daughters. As parents, we can't be asleep, and we can't do this alone. Like I mentioned at the outset, we need the Holy Spirit because victory ultimately comes from the Lord. With God's help and His strategy set in place, we can be effective in protecting our children against today's fiery arrows.

We will examine four fiery arrows that want to make our children casualties in the battle we fight. The adage "an enemy exposed is an enemy defeated" carries a lot of truth when it comes to raising tweens and teens in this day and age. God doesn't want us in the dark regarding the attacks that our children encounter. He wants us alongside our children in this battle. After examining these fiery darts, we'll look at safeguards that protect our children. These safeguards are found in God's Word, so the arrows in our hands can have the best chances of reaching the target that God has for them. Let's get started.

THE FIERY DART OF SOCIAL NETWORKING

Social networking is quite a popular thing for us today. Like millions of people, I love it. It's a great way to stay connected with friends and family near and far away. It can be used to encourage others, promote our faith, and even stay accountable in some instances. But with all the good comes a lot of bad—especially for young people. Leaders and parents should ask how this new phenomenon of social networking can be a fiery dart used by the enemy to divert children from their destiny.

Let's begin with an undeniable fact that most of us can admit to—social networking can be parasitical. For example, social networking has wasted millions of hours in the workplace, thus decreasing productivity in study and work. It has distracted limitless amounts of people, squashing their focus like a sumo wrestler sitting on a cup of Jell-O.

The effects that I see from social networking are that people can't focus on what's in front of them anymore—unless they have Internet capabilities, of course. I see this during preaching or when I go out to eat with others. We have all sat next to people who seemed a million miles away because of social networks and the Internet in general. As a result, some are programmed to have no attention span at all.

Some churchgoers surf the web during worship and the sermon. One question I like to ask young people is if they would be stuck to their phone if their future spouse was sharing their heart with them or possibly proposing to them. Sure, some may argue that the scenario isn't the same as church, but God's Word should hold a greater value in our hearts than those we dearly love.

Second, it negatively redefines family time—it eats up precious family time. Even the dinner table, which once meant family solidarity, has become nonexistent. Families are now online all the time. Even the former enforcers of family, moms and dads, are stuck on their tablets or smartphones. Even grandma has a social page, and she knows how to use it!

Although nothing is necessarily wrong with staying connected with others through social networking, danger lies in losing the authentic fabric of family. The foundation of strong families has always been built on the cornerstone of quality time. Social networking without restraint breaks that foundation. Kids are online, parents are online, and if there aren't boundaries and balance, things really get scary.

One can only guess intangible negatives of hypernetworking parents and their children. But there is one I can guarantee without assumption—the regret of wasted time. When we are on our deathbeds—hopefully in a very long time—we won't ask for our iPhones so we can update our Facebook status for people we hardly know and who frankly don't care about us. I don't know about you, but I will want my wife, kids, and close friends in the room with their undivided attention on me and my last words. And my last words aren't going to be, "I wish I would have spent more time online."

Third, it contributes to low self-esteem. Many young people look for approval and validation from outside the four walls of their homes through social networking. This is especially true of preteens and those from dysfunctional homes. These kids discover that they can't find what they're searching for online. They post comments and pictures, begging others for attention. And when no one shows interest in them, it can make low self-esteem lower.

Years ago, my wife and I were online when we noticed that a younger person was posting some comments in hopes of getting some sincere feedback and attention, but no one was responding. My wife did, and so did I, and then others responded. Thankfully, we showed this person that people care. Not every young person is that blessed. This shows the importance of parents and leaders being involved in the lives of their children when they are online because they desperately need our support, protection, and affirmation.

Lastly, it promotes narcissism. This is something that we can fail to consider. Of course, we want our children to have a healthy self-image. But on the other hand, we don't want them to go overboard. If you scroll through a social page of any young person, you'll usually find comments and pictures that are egoistic instead of meek. This contributes to a self-centered lifestyle in which everything revolves around a person rather than others. As a result, young people are constantly thinking about themselves, and a root of pride is given a wet environment to thrive in.

The Word exhorts us, "Do nothing out of selfish ambition or vain conceit, but in humility consider others better than yourselves. Each of you should look not only to your own interests, but also to the interests of others" (Philippians 2:3-4). Narcissism is like leprosy in the fingertips. The spiritual sense of touch is lost when selfishness consumes a soul. Paul knew that selfishness is the chief cause of waywardness.

You'll seldom find a humble prodigal, or more accurately, you never find a meek prodigal. That's why it's important to consider whether we are fostering a habit of narcissism in our children rather than a spirit of humility. With all the good that social networking has created, it must be used with balance and boundaries to be a blessing and not a curse. Is it a fiery dart that throws your kids off course, or is it directed, controlled, and aimed like an arrow in your hand? If God is involved, you'll be able to say yes to the latter.

THE FIERY DART OF EXCESSIVE TV

Doctors say that we are what we eat. I also believe that we are what we watch. If we take a good look at TV, we'll find that with the exception of Christian programming, God doesn't exist on mainstream TV. And when there is even a hint of Christianity, the media paints Christians as closed-minded morons who are hateful and hypocritical—a false stereotype indeed. This message has permeated Hollywood writers and producers since its inception. Christians are the bad guys and gals during prime-time TV. The laughingstock, the butt of all the jokes, the fools with a crutch—Christianity on TV is not Christianity at all. With everything we see on TV aimed at attacking our faith, you would think that Nero is calling the shots for TV stations.

Have you even noticed? The reason I ask is because one of the major side effects of watching excessive TV is that things that once bothered us no longer do. For example, do you remember the first time that you heard someone take God's name in vain on TV? Anger and hurt filled your heart because of the irreverence of God's name, as if the person was cursing at your father or mother. But that doesn't even faze many of us anymore.

What about when someone gets murdered? What happens when you see a sexually explicit reference or image—do you still turn your eyes and cover the kid's ears? The things that many once thought were totally wrong are now all right. Think about your position on highly debatable social issues. Have your morals changed in the last five years? Do they conform to Hollywood's ethic or God's standards?

Recently, I was cleaning my car with my youngest son. It's older and beat up a little, but when I first bought it, the car was spotless. In the early days, no food was allowed inside it. I even had to tell some friends that they couldn't bring food inside; needless to say, they didn't like that. But I can also say that it was always clean.

As time went on, things started to change. I began slipping in my standards of cleanliness in the car. One friend brought a soda and then a meal, and then as time went on, it got worse. I was no longer the young man with an immaculate vehicle. I was the guy who was embarrassed if you looked inside my vehicle. My standards had fallen.

That car is a good example of how convictions can be watered down or even lost when we conform to the world's standards—especially those from the media. Look at what Paul said on the matter: "Do not conform any longer to the pattern of this world, but be transformed by the renewing of your mind. Then you will be able to test and approve what God's will is—his good, pleasing and perfect will" (Romans 12:2).

Do those words mean the same to you as they did when you first read them? If not, there is a good possibility that your convictions are melting; you may have been conformed or desensitized. That very word connotes a subject that makes us feel very uncomfortable, but the truth, as Jesus poignantly said, will set us free (John 8:32).

In no way am I advocating that you throw out your flat screens and burn your satellite dishes. However, I am promoting that we start watching TV like Jesus is in the living room with us because He is. Just like I lost concern for my car, many people have lost the conviction of what they watch inside their home. And it's evident by how much time they spend in front of it and what they tune in to.

You might say, "I thought this was about kids watching excessive TV, not parents!" It is, but like I said before, parents set the patterns that kids follow. If you watch TV for hours, your kids will double the amount. If this is the case, we can take them to church for two hours a week, and there is a good possibility that they spend around twenty hours in front of a TV on any given week—if not more.

When kids watch TV, they're taught the world's gospel—a gospel that is the complete opposite of the Bible. That's why the TV can't be the babysitter or your child's teacher. Parents must set parameters around what their kids watch and how long they watch it. The wide road traveled by many prodigals was paved by Hollywood. What they see on the silver screen or the flat screen can be the greatest influence for them to abandon the faith. Without a doubt, TV is a powerful fiery dart in the hands of the enemy that has influenced and desensitized thousands of church kids and brought them to the dark side.

THE FIERY DART OF UNGODLY MUSIC

Music has a way of moving us to tears, uplifting our spirits, invoking our carnal desires, or bringing us back in time to a moment that transpired years before. Music has a profound way of influencing us. Most of my friends who left Christ had one common thread—their falling away commenced when they began listening to secular music, me included. Although there are many different views on this subject even within the Christian community, one thing is certain about popular secular music—it promotes a lifestyle antithetical of Christ.

For example, Green Day, one of the most famous punk bands of the last fifteen years, released a popular song titled "Jesus of Suburbia." The band sings about a young man who has lost all hope.[4] This song is blasphemous in the sense that it uses the Holy Scriptures and the very name of God's Son as metaphors for a hopeless person in a desperate condition. My question to Green Day is this: why use the name Jesus, whose very name is the essence of hope, who the writer of Hebrews describes as the blessed hope? Why bring the opposite of what you're writing about into the lyrics?

The answer can be found by watching MTV for less than five minutes, and it is that the god of this world controls music. Never in any other generation has God been mocked in music, downplayed in lyrics, or bashed in concerts more than in this generation. Anyone with a hint of common sense knows that music has a toxic effect on young people. When studying the crime scene of most prodigals, you'll find that music was a contributing factor in their downfall.

---

[4]   Green Day. *American Idiot.* Reprise Records 9362-48777-2, compact disc. Originally released in 2004.

And to make matters worse, there are some so-called Christian bands that are just as bad. Some stick to a Christian label simply because they can't make it in the mainstream. Then those who make it big dump their original beliefs like the teenage girl who dumps her younger boyfriend for the new heartthrob in town.

When I was a teen, a so-called Christian group that I liked stated on cable TV that they didn't want to be called Christians anymore. This isn't an isolated occurrence but more and more common. Many of these ambiguously Christian bands—a term that was coined by secular DJs, I might add—look just like any other secular bands. They have tattoos galore and body piercings that will make any underground punk rocker cringe. The only difference is that Christian teens can play them without their parents on their back because they carry a Christian label. But in essence, there's no difference between secular music and many of the so-called Christian bands.

Many people think that music can't affect a person or her beliefs or convictions. That is simply not true. Music defines us. Our values, attitudes, and purpose are closely connected to our playlists. When I was a teenager, I ran from God, and this fact really started showing itself when I began listening to grunge music. Before putting this book down or jumping to the next paragraph, hear me out.

Without my parents' approval (because they never allowed anything ungodly inside our home), I began listening to this grime. I also started being secretly creative, and with the crafty use of headphones, I downloaded garbage into my head—and it began to show. Depression commenced as I listened more.

Then I began smoking cigarettes, and then I began smoking marijuana, and then I even used LSD. I got more defiant toward God and my parents. If I wrote all the things I regret and all the people who I hurt by my actions during these dark times, it would be too painful to do. I was only sixteen years old, and I wanted to end my life. I wanted to die. I wanted to kill myself.

The floodgates of my rebellion began when I opened the door to worldly music. Do I have scientific evidence to back that statement? No. Am I 100 percent positive that I'm right? Yes. If you saw a picture of me back then and a picture of me now, you would see a different person. This might sound a little corny, but I'm just being honest. And if we take a truthful look at secular and ambiguously Christian music, we'll both come to the same conclusion.

Do you feel like living a holy life after listening to Marilyn Manson, or do you feel like living in rebellion toward God? Did you think that you invited the Holy Spirit into your room when you played Black Sabbath as a teenager? Or did it feel more like you were summoning demons? So why would it be different for your child? I didn't feel like God had an awesome plan for my life when I listened to Kurt Cobain when my parents were out of the house. No,

I felt like doing the same thing that he did in real life. I wanted to kill myself.

Okay, perhaps you're saying that those are devil groups and that your kids would never listen to that garbage. They just listen to the normal stuff—the kid channel stuff—the stuff that you hear at the roller skating rink. My rebuttal to that is to ask if you have listened closely to that stuff lately. Even all the normal stuff is tainted. The typical stuff is full of sexual innuendos that encourage lives of promiscuity among young girls and guys.

Case in point—one of the more popular artists, Katy Perry, sings, "I want to see your peacock."[5] Tell me if I'm wrong, but I don't think she is referring to a bird. And in another song, she sings, "I kissed a girl, and I liked it."[6] There's nothing ambiguous about that statement. Perry has a massive following—particularly among young girls. She is seen at all the kids' music awards with standing ovations from kids and parents alike. Perry is the carbon copy of many mainstream artists who sing with abstract defiance to the things of God. The new normal isn't like the old normal; this stuff is abnormal.

Truly, music is intoxicating. It hinders some from letting go and moving on. That's what it did to me. At times, I wanted to surrender to God, but I couldn't until I

---

[5]   Katy Perry. *Teenage Dream.* Capitol Records 5099972963425, compact disc. Originally released in 2010.
[6]   Katy Perry. *One of the Boys.* Capitol Records 5099950424924, compact disc. Originally released in 2008.

surrendered my collection of worldly music to God. It was my roadblock, hindering passage to the light. Even now, I talk to many young adults and parents who think that it's perfectly fine to listen to this secular music. The evidence of their lives shows that ungodly music is a powerful fiery dart that can affect us immensely.

THE FIERY DART OF PORN

Porn is a growing epidemic in every institution that God ordained, such as marriage and the family. It's an even greater threat for today's generation than past generations because of its easy accessibility via the Internet. Teens no longer have to walk across town and be sneaky to view it. From the comfort of their own computers, phones, or tablets, they can be entangled by a multibillion-dollar industry that God's Word clearly forbids.

With just the click of a button, kids can enter a world of countless sexually explicit images and videos that would take more than their entire lifetime to view if they looked at it continuously because of the enormity of the business. One recent study stated the following:

- Forty million Americans regularly visit porn sites.
- Seventy percent of men between the ages of eighteen and twenty-four visit porn sites in a typical month.
- One in three porn viewers are women.
- One in four search engine requests are porn-related.

- The most popular day of the week for viewing porn is Sunday.
- The average age at which a child first sees porn online is eleven.[7]

Sadly, many young men and women are addicted. When I was a student, I clearly heard one man say that pornography is more addictive than crack cocaine. For many people, this statement is a reality. And like smoking, it's a habit that usually starts early. The enemy knows that if people can be hooked when they're young, they can be slaves for life. Taking a look at porn's side effects on young people is sobering.

First, it desensitizes kids to God's plan of sexual purity. God has given each one of us conviction. This is particularly true for young people. Their minds can be called pure, pliable, and impressionable. So when an eleven-year-old starts viewing porn, the purity is out the door, and an impression of sexual waywardness begins. The more this young person looks at porn, the more he becomes affected by it. He goes from one extreme to the next—from a mind of purity to a mind of promiscuity. With every passing day that this fiery dart goes unchecked or unexposed, the mind becomes more twisted and perverted. The mind becomes more desensitized to God's purpose of purity.

---

[7] Publicity. "Internet Pornography Stats." Last modified June 22, 2010. http://www.publiciti.ru/en/digest/internet-pornography-stats.

Second, it undermines God's institution of marriage. Consequently, porn can be deemed anti-marriage. The reasons are as plain as day. It promotes pleasure rather than commitment. It's an advocate of lust instead of love, and it pushes sexual promiscuity rather than God's design of sexual exclusivity between one man and one woman for their lifetime. The bottom line is that it endorses selfishness as a substitute for selflessness. Commitment, love, and sexual exclusivity are chief cornerstones of marriage. On the other hand, selfishness, sexual promiscuity, and lust are the chief enemies of marriage.

Third, it creates a warped view of sex. One area in which you'll find porn affecting various young people today is the way they view and perform sex. Many are enslaved to lives of masturbation, trying to live out what they seen on the Internet from people who are disease-infected and money-driven. No doubt, these so-called porn stars read scripts that are delivered from the depths of hell. This industry ruins people's perception of sex and also their sex lives, because sin brings death to every institution that God desires to bless.

Sex was created to be special and a blessing between a husband and his wife. Now the word *sex* connotes something negative because of what people are exposed to by the porn business. Sex is now synonymous with dirt, sleaze, and impurity. The sex lives of many young men and women have been ruined because they have been so twisted by this fiery dart.

This is a far cry from God's original plan, which was (and still is) beautiful and pure in every facet. Porn is a powerful fiery dart which has its sights set on the eyes and hearts of our children. Only with God's help can we effectively protect and prepare our children for this dart when it is launched their way.

SAFEGUARDS AGAINST THE ENEMY

Last, I want to look at some safeguards that will help us in this battle for our children. All of them carry applications which help us abate these four fiery darts and all the other flaming arrows that I didn't mention. With God's help, the following safeguards, and the wisdom of our spiritual leaders, we can build an effective strategy against the plans of the enemy. Let's make this happen!

- First and foremost, we need God. I cannot stress enough the importance of seeking God with these issues. The supernatural strength and wisdom of God is necessary if we are going to be victorious in this battle. If parents don't have a personal and thriving relationship with the Lord, they will fail to follow the direction of the Holy Spirit. God must come first, and everything else should be secondary. This is the attitude that we must have, because with it, we'll be on guard against the fiery darts that come toward us and our kids.

- We must shower our kids with prayer. Prayer is our greatest asset that helps us protect our children against the fiery arrows of the enemy. At night, when my children are asleep, I get up and lay hands on their heads, just praying whatever I have in my heart. During the day, when they pop into my head, I pray for them again, asking the Lord to protect them and use them as He sees fit. It's a practice that was handed down from my parents. This made a lasting impact on my life and gave me a pattern that I still follow today.

- Surprise your children with a random visit to their rooms, computers, and cell phones. When was the last time you looked in your child's stuff? It's funny how many young people demand privacy as policy. Guess what? You're the parent, and as long as your children live in your house, grant them none! Surprise them with random visits whenever the Spirit prompts you to do so. Doing this will make them think twice before they do something that you don't allow.

- Be aware of their friends online. With the onslaught of criminal activity, predators, and negative influences. Parents have to be fully aware of who their kids associate with online. Looking through your child's social page is good parenting. The web is lurking with predators who are on the hunt for any naïve preteens and teenagers to victimize. Many have alter egos and project themselves as handsome young men or beautiful women when they are really older, ugly perverts from who-knows-where.

In 2009, a convicted sex offender by the name of Peter Chapman used the fake identity of a teenage boy to entice a seventeen-year-old girl named Ashleigh Hall to meet him. After raping her, he viciously killed her. How did this tragedy happen? Well, he created a fake profile on Facebook and used pictures of a boy in his late teens to fool her into meeting him in a remote location. Ashleigh's mother said, "She wasn't naughty. She made one mistake and has paid for it with her life."[8] That story is a sobering reminder that as parents, we must always be on guard in our children's social networking lives.

- Place time restraints on them. A child without limits will live a life without limits. This is pretty basic but true. A teen who doesn't have online boundaries is a ticking time bomb. And when it blows, it isn't going to be pretty. A good rule of thumb is that a child's time online should not exceed his devotional time with God.

  This is true for parents, too! Talk about a major incentive for them to pray! If parents enforced this, teens all across the country would turn into

8   The Guardian. "Facebook killer sentenced to life for teenager's murder." Last modified March 8, 2010. http://www.guardian.co.uk/uk/2010/mar/08/peter-chapman-facebook-killer.

intercessors! It's feasible if parents do their part. Think about it—who wrote the book that rules and regulations don't apply to teenagers anymore? I call rules pointing the arrows that God has entrusted to you in the right direction. Both sides must understand that social networking is a privilege, not a right. As parents, we are stewards of our children. In return, our children are stewards of what we entrust to their care, including social networking.

If a teen can't handle the privilege of social networking in a responsible matter, then disconnection from social networking is warranted. The reasons for disconnecting are easily noticed, such as a drop in grades, bad attitude, posting unethical statements or images, and being negatively influenced by others online. Conversely, the reasons to allow them to be connected via social networking are pretty obvious—good grades, a good attitude, and content that does not cross any boundaries.

Ultimately, the decision to allow a young person to have a social account lies in the lap of a parent's intuition. Recently, my wife and I talked to a mom who disconnected her teen's Facebook account. She noticed some red flags and took a bold step against the grain of today's culture in deactivating her child's account. Kudos to her as a parent. Today both mother and daughter are doing great. This goes to show that a teenager's life will not end as a result of not being connected online. It might actually do a teen some good.

- Address the dangers. For instance, porn is a joke to everyone in media. Hollywood takes a lighthearted and childish approach to a dangerous subject. I can also guarantee that in every other arena of your child's life, they will also take this fallacious approach—with the exception of the church. Parents must vocalize the dangers that porn and every other fiery dart that we looked at can bring in the lives of our children. Fathers and mothers shouldn't shy away from this subject but rather attack it as frequently as the Lord leads. Warn your child of the dangers that these darts pose to her future. Don't just leave it up to the church to do all the dirty work.

- Set the example that you want your kids to follow. What we do when our children watch and when they don't watch sets the model that they'll follow. Fathers and mothers must be a cut above. Although the enemy points fiery darts at your children, it has twice as many arrows aimed at parents—especially fathers—because of the collateral damage that follows. Remember, our children are like arrows in our hands. Which direction are our hands pointed?

Conclusion

As parents, we are called to protect our children. This means that we won't be popular at times, but God's Word doesn't tell us to live to please our children. Rather, it tells us to live to please Him. This is a mandate from the Lord, and regardless of what other parents allow their kids to partake in, we can't lose godly conviction.

Our children are arrows in our hands. This is a great responsibility but also a tremendous privilege. We point our children through our actions, words, and attitudes. It's pretty obvious that good parents and role models are in short supply today. We're living in a tough world, and building a Christian family is harder than it was just five years ago. But it's not impossible when God's leads and we as parents follow His voice.

FOR PRODIGALS ONLY

If you're not a prodigal, this chapter might not make any sense to you, so proceed carefully.

What made you leave Christ? That's one question that you'll usually find a lengthy, diverse, and sometimes nebulous answer to. My reason, your reason, and any prodigal's reason for abandoning the faith that was handed down to us by parents never come without some drama.

Most of us sound like lawyers in a courtroom, passionately defending ourselves in front of jurors who will decide our eternal fate. We argue, rationalize, and present our cases. But can our arguments really convince God that we're right in leaving Him? And for that matter, can we truly persuade ourselves that we are fine without Him? More importantly, are the reasons for leaving God really worth a life without Him? These are significant questions that should be considered—weighed with an open heart and looked upon with open eyes.

Let's have a debate. You can present your argument on why you're not serving Christ any longer. Then I'll present my reasons I believe you should return. You can begin; you have my attention. Court is in session!

Your Argument

- *I'm just too busy right now. Maybe when I get some more time, I'll drop by.* With all the things going on in my life today, I just don't have the time. But when it slows down, you might see me back.

- *I'm not ready to come back yet, but someday, I will be.* Sooner or later, I want to return, but I'm just not ready to do that. I know that what I'm doing is wrong, but it's nearly impossible for me to give it up right now.

- *My lifestyle is clearly wrong according to the Bible, and I don't see myself giving it up.* I've just learned to live my life the way that I'm going to live it. I'm not going to change it so I can conform to something I learned back in Sunday school.

- *I'm doing fine without Christ in my life. Why should I return?* Things are going great. I'm happy, satisfied, and just living my life. All the stuff about being miserable away from God doesn't seem to apply to me.

- *I've been hurt so badly in church.* The things that happened to me and my family at church deeply wounded me, and I'm not coming back.

- *I don't believe in God anymore.* I've come to see things differently than I did as a child. I look at things with a rational outlook, not a religious one.

Thank you for expressing your thoughts and reasons for leaving God. But before you put this book down and go on with your life, I ask that you hear me out for the next five minutes or so. I challenge you to listen with an open heart.

MY CASE

Let me begin by saying that I was a prodigal myself. Some of the points that you've expressed were also my beliefs. But the more I considered the evidence with an open heart, the more I was drawn to return to Christ. I'm going to present several critical factors or reasons that will hopefully make you reconsider your choice to leave God. Carefully listen to what I'm going to say, because so much hinges on your choice to serve Christ or not—more than any of us can imagine. Let's begin!

THE EXPERIENCE FACTOR

A majority of you were sincerely touched by God, but now it seems that you have a case of spiritual amnesia when it comes to everything that Christ has shown you in the past. Many of you have experienced firsthand the love of God. But doubt, unbelief, and deception have stolen those experiences away from you. This is vital, because when someone authentically encounters Jesus, something happens. These experiences stay with us for life. Prodigals who once experienced God are like people who survive a bolt of lightning.

Years ago, I had a dear friend who I grew up with. We did everything together. When we got older, we both slipped away from God. I eventually returned to Christ, but he didn't. We were still friends, but things were obviously not the same. When I told him about my change of heart, he told me that he was an atheist. At the tail end of high school, he was in a terrible accident and nearly died! When I went to visit him in the hospital, he couldn't even respond.

Weeks went by, and my friend finally became coherent again. He told us that while he was unconscious, he went to hell. After that encounter, I never heard him doubt the existence of God and the supernatural again. I believe this encounter happened to him for two reasons. First, God wanted to show him how much He loved him, and second, God wanted to warn him of the road he was traveling. But in spite of this close brush with death, we are still praying for him to completely surrender to Christ.

Encounters with God are powerful reminders of His mercy and grace. They all point to a Savior who desperately loves His children and is willing to manifest Himself to them. These experiences must be viewed through the eyes of faith and looked upon for what they truly are—proof that He loves us. Don't forget that.

THE DOMINO FACTOR

All of us know that our choices influence others. But we must really think about how when one of us turns from God, it doesn't just impinge on us alone, but it also negatively affects those who are closest to us, such as our parents, siblings, and friends.

A majority of prodigals fail to examine the domino effect of their choices. Sadly, in many cases, prodigals only think about one person in the equation—themselves. Narcissism blinds them to the investment of their parents, the sacrifices of their leaders, and vulnerability of their siblings.

Although many of you are ashamed of your mistakes, you must also be mindful of the positive effects that will arise from your return to Christ. For instance, can you imagine the joy that would fill your mother's heart if she heard that her son rededicated his life back to God or that her daughter was coming back to Lord? Nothing in the entire world would bring a parent more excitement! Think about that!

THE HURT FACTOR

Out of all the reasons for leaving Christ, this one is the most common, because Christians are to act and live a certain way. But sometimes we'll find people—even in God's house—who live contrary to what they profess and claim they believe.

Not too long ago, one young man I know was arrested, and his mugshot was printed in our local newspaper. He was involved in a shameful crime that I'm sure he wished he never committed. Years earlier, he was actively going to church, and for the most part didn't show any signs of leaving. Finally, right around the age of eighteen, he left Christ and fell hard.

When I talked to this young man about his reasons for leaving, he stated he left because of a person who had hurt him in church years before. The hurt was legitimate, but it was not grounds for leaving God—nothing ever is. The enemy had used this offense to hinder him from his destiny.

This is what many of you have probably faced also. Such as people failing you—or even worse, failing God. Some terrible things have happened to me, too. I can sympathize with many of you. Some of those hurts made me question everything—including God—because they were embarrassing and devastating.

But if I let all the bad things that happened to me and my family control my emotions, I would've left God a long time ago. Looking back, I'm very glad I didn't, because I would've lost many blessings, and I wouldn't have seen God heal the deep wounds within my life and in lives of those closest to me. These are things that would've been completely destroyed if I let the mistakes of others ruin my perception of Christ. When you weigh it out, the benefits of forgiving those who have hurt us always are greater than holding on to unforgiveness. This is something to think about. Holding on to past hurts will hinder us from a bright future with Christ.

THE TOO-LATE FACTOR

Have you ever felt like it's too late to come back to Christ? Or even worse, do you believe that you have done too many bad things to deserve His forgiveness?

We can waste valuable time running from God, but as long as we're breathing, it not too late. After we're dead, it is. And we can never deserve forgiveness from our own good deeds; it's a free gift that comes as a result of God's grace to us. The Bible says, "For it is by grace you have been saved, through faith—and this not from yourselves, it is the gift of God—not by works, so that no one can boast" (Ephesians 2:8-9).

People always try to earn what they get. Do this and this, and the results should be this and that. But God's grace is something that isn't contingent on what we do; it hinges completely on what Christ already did on the cross. Prodigals often tell me things like, "I'm going to give my life back to Christ after I start living right." I understand what they're trying to say, but the problem with that type of thinking is that they're trying to earn grace—something that's impossible to do. Even our best works are like filthy rags in comparison with God's holiness. Our best works still demanded God's best—His one and only Son, Jesus.

If you think it's too late, it isn't, and if you feel that you have done too many sinful things to ever be forgiven, you're wrong. Grace is greater than our past, and those who surrender to God's grace in faith have an awesome future in Christ.

THE TIME FACTOR

Time doesn't put on the brakes for any of us. Our lives are like a thirty-second TV commercial; they fly right by the screen we call eternity. We have one moment—one chance—to make this thing count.

Some time ago, I was driving home on a narrow, two-lane road when a tired or drunk driver swerved into my lane. I was going nearly sixty miles per hour. I hit the brakes and lost control of my car. I was headed straight for the oncoming car, but thankfully, my car slipped to the side of the road just before impact. When I arrived home, I just thanked God for another day! Looking at my kids and seeing my wife welcome me home was priceless because time is priceless! What happened to me that night made me really consider death, because after we die, the following will occur:

- We will give an answer for everything that we have done—all the way down to every careless word that we have said (Romans 14:12).
- We will be appointed our eternal home—heaven or hell (Revelation 21:27).

I'm not trying to be morbid, but are you ready to die? Many prodigals argue that the afterlife is not real. Do you really believe that, or are you just attempting to pacify your fears? Don't gamble with the devil. Where we are going to spend eternity depends on us. Why risk your soul for the temporal pleasures of sin? This is something that you can't play with, because you don't know if today is your last day to live. Someday, that last day will come.

Closing Argument

One thing that irritates all of us is when we don't have a chance or an opportunity to prove ourselves. For instance, do you remember when you played sports as a kid? Before the game, the captains of each team picked sides. Were you ever the kid who didn't get picked on the team—you know, the skinny kid who didn't get a chance to show that he or she could play because of size or appearance? That's how many prodigals treat God. They pick everything else and choose Christ when they have nothing else to choose. Like the little kid who doesn't get picked, Jesus is overlooked, and other things or people are chosen instead.

It seems that the simplicity of the gospel is too much for many prodigals to believe. They want to complicate the matter, theorize their opinions of Jesus, and brush Him off like the little kid who never got a chance.

Then some fail to encounter Jesus, because when He touches them with His love, they still hold on to their sins without turning away from them. They miss the open door and take the grace and mercy of God lightly. As a result, they are stuck in perpetual ruts, oblivious to the reasons they can't break free. It wasn't that Christ lost His power; it's that they failed to do their part when they had the chance.

Jesus will open the door for all of us to escape destruction, but He'll never force us through that door. We have to walk through on our own. You and I have the choice; we pick which way we go. Many of us have made all the wrong choices because we haven't chosen Jesus.

How is your life without Christ working for you? Are you too proud to admit that you're empty? Could it be possible that your parents, pastors, and godly friends were right all along in telling you that Christ Jesus is the way, the truth, and the life? Were those feelings that you felt as a child more than your emotions getting the best of you?

The answer is yes.

Christ is the truth. The most important person that you'll ever need to meet is Him. Even if you walked away from Him before, He still loves you and is willing to forgive you. He wants to see you come home. I'm not going to lie and say that it's going to be easy, because He asks for everything. But if you give Him everything, the things you give up won't compare with what He gives you in return. So what are you going to do? Are you coming home, or are you going to live in the pig's pen for the rest of your life?

The choice is yours.

PRODIGAL'S PRAYER

Lord, forgive me for what I've done. I'm so sorry for breaking your heart. My actions and mistakes have brought guilt and shame in my life. I'm tired of running. Right now, I ask that you please forgive me! Create in me a clean heart, and renew a right spirit within me. Break all the chains of the enemy in my life by the power of your blood. All this I ask in Jesus' name.

Welcome home!

Heaven's Heroes

Therefore, my dear brothers, stand firm. Let nothing
move you. Always give yourselves fully to the work of the
Lord, because you know that your labor in the Lord is not
in vain. 1 Corinthians 15:58

H EAVEN HAS A SPECIAL PLACE for parents, pastors, and
friends who never gave up on their prodigals. Yes,
my friend, these people are the heroes of heaven. These are
champions who fought on their knees in prayer during the
dark and cold times that life unfairly brings. These heroes
are men and women both young and old who knew what
it is to cry until empty of tears. Accustomed to heartbreak,
they never let it break their hope in God's promises.

These relentless warriors are you and I—ordinary
people with everyday jobs and responsibilities who are
extraordinary in the sense that without them, the streets
of heaven wouldn't be filled with the people we love.
Fearlessly, they stand before the gates of hell, pressing
through in prayer for their sons and daughters. They fight
for the souls and destinies of their children against the
hordes of hell's mightiest. And by the strength and grace
of God, these heroes prevail!

Most certainly, this isn't a task for the fainthearted. In every aspect, it's a job that our hearts can't sustain on willpower or muster up by mere good intentions. The heart of a hero is a heart that only God can give. It requires a divine download of His grace and strength and the empowerment of His Spirit. It's cultivated in the fertile ground of determination and unyielding trust in the promises of God. Right now, we are going to examine these qualities as we look together at a heart of a hero.

HEAVEN'S HEROES NEVER QUIT FIGHTING

A tenacious spirit is in the heart of all heroes. It drives them to fight when discouraged and wounded in spirit. In spite of circumstances, they are like a bulldog with a bone. They will not let go. They never quit fighting because

- they understand that others won't fight for their children with the same passion,
- they want to see God's best for their kids,
- they are deeply concerned about the eternal direction their children are going,

These are the factors that fuel their fire. All the parents who have been victorious in this fight let these elements motivate them to pay a heavy price.

Fasting and prayer were things that became part of these parents' lifestyles. Instead of dwelling in a comfort zone of inactivity, they lived in battle zones that many would run from. I have witnessed parents who all the odds worked against, but they continued to fight for their children. And now their kids are serving God.

The return of their son or daughter was never instantaneous. It's not like they said a little prayer for their prodigals, and lo and behold, their kids knocked at the front door, asking their parents to lead them in the sinner's prayer. No, the truth is that for some of these heroes, a child's return took years. But that made the child's homecoming so much sweeter. When we fully grasp this, it encourages us in the next place we'll explore.

Heroes Stand in the Gap

Another thing that is true of the heroes of heaven is that they stand in the gap. The prophet Ezekiel wrote, "I looked for a man among them who would build up the wall and stand before me in the gap on behalf of the land so I would not have to destroy it, but I found none" (Ezekiel 22:30).

In the scriptural context of Ezekiel 22:30, the term "stand in the gap" means to implore God's mercy on behalf of another person. During Ezekiel's day, God looked for a man or woman who would seek His mercy for the nation of Israel. But none could be found. Heroes continuously beseech the mercies of God for their prodigals.

I'm very thankful that during my teenage years, my parents stood in the gap for me, because the road I was traveling was extremely destructive. I wouldn't cross out the possibility of being dead if they hadn't stood in the gap. But I had two superheroes who prayed for my salvation and for the mercy of God on my behalf.

My parents cried numerous tears for my salvation and protection. I vividly remember walking by their room in the morning and hearing my mother praying for me when I was a teenager. This shifted the whole course of my life in a positive way because without her standing in the gap for me, I'm certain of the person I would be today. I know the negative direction I was headed.

Heroes create a bridge of prayer on which prodigals can walk from death to life, from guilt to grace, and from sin to salvation. My parents' prayers were my bridge over the gap that sin created in my life. Without their prayers, the gap would have only gotten bigger, and I would have slipped further into darkness.

When parents and leaders stand in the gap, something powerful happens. It's almost as though the person you pray for is dying in the middle of nowhere, and there's no one to help. But you are there, and you are keeping them alive so they won't pass the brink of no return. It's like you call out for help to God because he or she can't. Standing in the gap is a heavy task, and those who stand there faithfully and fervently will be rewarded!

Heaven's Heroes Will Be Rewarded

One of the most encouraging things I see is when people get recompensed for doing the right thing. As a kid, I watched an old TV show that rewarded people for doing good deeds, and many were thought to be unseen. For instance, the producers of the show left a wallet full of cash and credit cards in a shopping basket at a grocery store with hidden cameras recording. Every once in a while, you'd find an honest citizen who would return the wallet, and when the person returned it, the producers and camera crew came out from behind the scenes and gave the good standing citizen a financial reward. They questioned the people about why they did what they did. Their usual response was, "I knew I had to do the right thing."

We all wish it was this easy, right? Do the right things, get the right reward! But we can rest assured that heaven's cameras are rolling. God see everything. And for that reason, He rewards everything. Solomon put it like this in Proverbs 11:18: "The wicked man earns deceptive wages, but he who sows righteousness reaps a sure reward."

God isn't a cheapskate who is running low on faith funds. Our God is the most generous boss we ever will work for. And if we sow into the lives of our unsaved loved ones, we will get a sure reward. The check is in the mail, so to speak. God has a blessing for all your stressing! Paul said, "Let us not become weary in doing good, for at the proper time we will reap a harvest if we do not give up" (Galatians 6:9).

Don't think for one moment that God doesn't see your tears for your daughter! Don't second guess your sacrifice and prayers for your unsaved son. Don't doubt in your heart that God is going to pass you by. Don't lose faith! God is going to reward you. Maybe it's today or maybe ten years from now. Perhaps it's five months from this day, or maybe you're going to witness your child's return five years from now. The bottom line is that you can't lose heart because you have rewards in store!

When we get to heaven, God will reward each of us for the sacrifices we made. The Bible says that books will be opened, and every deed we ever committed is recorded (Revelation 20:12). This image makes me think about parents with prodigals, standing before the throne. In front of innumerable witnesses, the books of heaven will be opened for you, and God Himself will show everyone what you have done.

I see mothers who wept for their wayward daughters standing before the throne! I see pastors who endured the agony of ministering the gospel while their sons turned away from the truth. They pushed past the brink of hopelessness. They were not victims to the chains of unbelief. They stood firm until the end. I have seen the passion in their eyes, the fight in their fists, and the callouses on their knees. I see parents who never let go but held on to God's promise in Proverbs 22:6: "Train a child in the way he should go, and when he is old he will not turn from it."

This verse gives us reason to hope and believe. God placed this Scripture in His Word because He knew that there would be children like yours, stuck in a life of rebellion and sin—but He also wanted us know these chains can be broken! When you look back at Proverbs 22:6, it's evident that your investment in your children is the sledgehammer that's going to break every chain. It's what you already did; it's what you showed, taught, and modeled to them as they were in your care.

Conclusion

In March of 2012, I was privileged to go on a mission trip with my wife. At one church, I was given the opportunity to share my story of how I was a prodigal pastor's kid who came back to the Lord. After the service, a woman came up to my wife and me and told us that my testimony really encouraged her because two of her sons also left God. When I saw the desperation in her eyes, God confirmed the need for the book that I had been working on for years before we met.

On many other occasions, I came across people who were in the same predicament as this woman. They gave me the same message. When this happened it was like a lighthouse in the night, guiding the direction of this book.

There were many times I wanted to quit this project or simply write about another topic. I knew that some would think I was unqualified, and others would think that I was just being idealistic about a problem that I was once a part of. But my heart was always driven back to the subject of prodigals. The more that I wrestled with God, the more He confirmed what He wanted me to write about with encounters like the one I just mentioned.

This is what pushed me to march on. God knew that some of you needed to hope again. He was fully cognizant of how my humble story would inspire some of you to still believe that your son or daughter could come back too. I finally came to realize that this was never my project; this was God's project. When that happened, I knew I had to move out of the way and let Him have His way. So I boldly say, believe, hero!

"This is what the Lord says: 'Restrain your voice from weeping and your eyes from tears, for your work will be rewarded,' declares the Lord. 'They will return from the land of the enemy. So there is hope for your future,' declares the Lord. 'Your children will return to their own land'" (Jeremiah 31:16-17).

Danny Casas Jr.

About the Author

Danny Casas Jr. is a pastor and youth speaker who specializes in ministering to teenagers and parents alike. Since 2007, he has led New Harvest Christian Fellowship of Porterville, California. His passion is found in the book of Malachi 4:6: "To see God turn the hearts of the fathers to their children, and the hearts of children to their fathers." Danny and his lovely wife, Sabrina, live in central California with their four children.

Learn more at *eyesofaprodigal.com.*